The Westons

PRESENTED TO

Mike Yorkey

FROM

July 27, 2002

DATE

IN HIS COURT

BETSY NAGELSEN McCORMACK

with Mike Yorkey

COUNTRYMAN

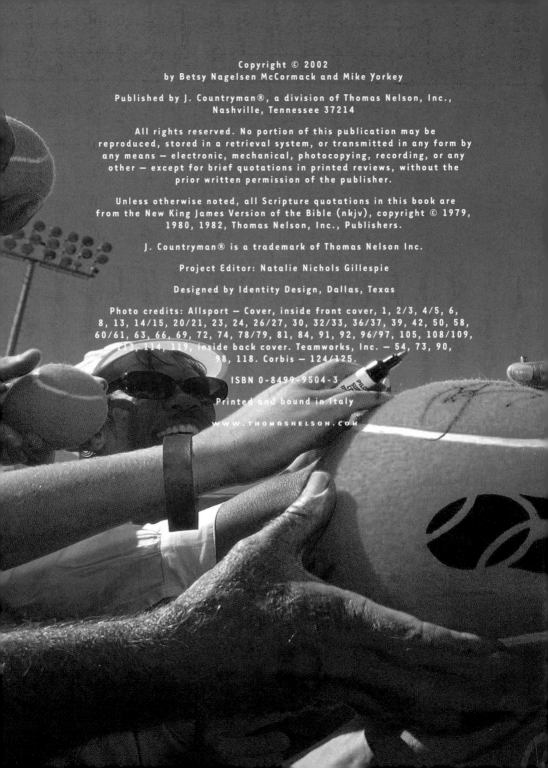

Unless otherwise noted, all Scripture quotations in this book are
from the New King James Version of the Bible (nkjv), copyright © 1979,
1980, 1982, Thomas Nelson, Inc., Publishers.

J. Countryman® is a trademark of Thomas Nelson Inc.

Project Editor: Natalie Nichols Gillespie

Designed by Identity Design, Dallas, Texas

Photo credits: Allsport — Cover, inside front cover, 1, 2/3, 4/5, 6,
8, 13, 14/15, 20/21, 23, 24, 26/27, 30, 32/33, 36/37, 39, 42, 50, 58,
60/61, 63, 66, 69, 72, 74, 78/79, 81, 84, 91, 92, 96/97, 105, 108/109,
113, 114, 119, inside back cover. Teamworks, Inc. — 54, 73, 90,
98, 118. Corbis — 124/125.

ISBN 0-8499-9504-3

Printed and bound in Italy

WWW.THOMASNELSON.COM

TABLE OF CONTENTS

To Mom, for giving me my love for tennis and for giving me my love for God. I would also like to dedicate this book to my little daughter, MAGGIE, who has been truly a miracle gift from God, and who has shown me the real meaning of the word "love." I hope these pages will help you continue to grow in God's image and understanding of His love for you.

ACKNOWLEDGEMENTS

The completion of this book would not have been possible without the help of:

• My parents, who raised me with Christian values that have become ever more important as the years have gone by.

• My husband, MARK, whose extraordinary memory helped recall tennis history and milestones in my tennis career.

• SARA TROLLINGER, whose spiritual guidance and Christian walk have been such an inspiration to me.

• JILL SMICHERKO, whose tireless efforts and ongoing persistence kept me on track.

• MIKE YORKEY, my co-writer on the project, who put up with chasing me around the world and hours of phone calls at times that were certainly more convenient for me than for him. Also, thanks to Sara Trollinger's sister, Jane Chambers, and Lynette Winkler of Spiez, Switzerland, for reading earlier versions of this manuscript.

FOREWORD
BY MONICA SELES

If you've followed tennis for the past few years, you've probably heard the reports of how I was suddenly attacked during a 1993 tournament in Hamburg, Germany. A spectator reached out from the stands and plunged a knife into my back. The unexpected assault changed my world in an instant. I retreated to my Florida home and sheltered myself from the world.

As the months passed, there was one constant light that shone through that dark period: Betsy McCormack. She phoned. She visited. She said she was praying for me. She asked whether there was anything that she could do for me. She loved me unconditionally. Betsy didn't care if I ever picked up a tennis racket again. I found out she would be there for me no matter what the future brought.

One summer day about eighteen months after the stabbing, I dropped by Betsy's home in Orlando, Florida, to say hello. I hadn't hit a tennis ball since Hamburg. Betsy was playing on her backyard court, hitting away with a partner. They looked like they were having fun. On a whim, I asked, "Mind if I join in?"

"Of course," replied Betsy, who walked over to her racket bag and handed me one of hers. Then we realized I wasn't wearing tennis shoes! We giggled like schoolgirls when I stepped out of my flats and walked onto the court barefoot. I was going to hit my first ball since that tragic day without wearing any tennis shoes! She didn't care, and neither did I. We stood side by side on the baseline and began hitting forehands and backhands with her hitting partner. As I met the ball with the racket and sent it back on a line over the net, it all started coming back to me. I could still play! I could still hit the ball!

That afternoon, Betsy helped me realize how much I missed the game I had grown to love. She also did something even greater. She shared several Psalms with me at a Bible study at her house — Psalms that gave me encouragement.

Throughout this book, Betsy shares other Scriptures and how they relate to the game we both love. She is one of the most gracious people I know, and it comes across clearly in these pages. Betsy is the type of person who would give you the tennis shirt off her back. Isn't there a lesson in the Bible about that?

INTRODUCTION
BY MICHAEL CHANG

If you've ever seen me play tennis, you know that I'm a battler on the court. My game is based on consistency and counterpunching, not blazing serves or big forehands. I'm always playing someone bigger and stronger, which means I have to move my opponent from corner to corner, exploit angles, and take his speed and send it right back at him.

I've always persevered on the tennis court, through good times and bad. My greatest comeback happened at the 1989 French Open when I was just seventeen. I came from two sets down to defeat Ivan Lendl and continue on my way to my first Grand Slam victory. You'll read more about that match later in these pages. On the downside, I fought for five hours and twenty-six minutes against Stefan Edberg in the 1992 U.S. Open semifinals — the longest match in U.S. Open history — but left Louis Armstrong Court with a bitter defeat.

In each situation, I've learned to lean on Jesus Christ, my source of inspiration. Just as I've fought to persevere on the tennis court, I've also fought to persevere in my Christian life. My walk with Christ is a five-set match, not a twelve-point tiebreaker, and I'm going to follow Him until the end of my days.

I'm also trying to lead a life worthy of Him. Back home in the Seattle area, I keep my nineteen-foot walleye bass boat — named "Fisher of Men" — ready to go when I'm home for a spell. I'm a fishing fanatic who loves being on the water with a fishing rod in hand, fishing for small mouth bass and sockeye salmon when they're running.

"Fisher of Men" is an apt name for my boat because it's been my great hope that my tennis career, playing in front of thousands of people and before millions on TV, has helped me be a "fisher of men." If I've been able to draw people to the Lord through my tennis, the fame and the money and the rankings won't compare to touching people's lives and encouraging them in the Lord. That's something that lasts a lifetime and beyond.

And that's why you're going to like *In His Court*. Betsy McCormack has served up quite a book, which means that you're going to enjoy yourself and be encouraged as you read this beautifully produced volume of inspiration and hope based on the great game of tennis.

In His Court tells great stories from tennis' colorful past and offers spiritual points that we can all take to heart. You'll be glad you wet a line by the time you're finished.

PREFACE
BY BETSY NAGELSEN McCORMACK

"Tennis, anyone?"

That silly question entered the American lexicon back in the days when tennis was played by men in boaters and cream-colored pants and women bound by whale-boned corsets who tiptoed around the court In full-length skirts and long-sleeve shirts. "Tennis, anyone?" seems as antiquated as wooden presses and white tennis sweaters trimmed in burgundy and navy blue.

These days, a more apt phrase would be "Tennis, everyone?" More than twenty million Americans play tennis regularly on public courts in parks, high schools, community colleges, and neighborhoods and at private clubs. Although tennis as we know it began 125 years ago as a party game played on the expansive lawns of the English upper crust, the game has evolved into an egalitarian sport open to all.

These days, the cost to play is rather modest. Rackets made from Space Age materials such as graphite and kevlar can be purchased for under $100, while used rackets cost a fraction of that price. A pair of sneakers, a $3 can of balls, and a tennis court are all it takes to play today. Some recreational players choose to join private tennis clubs and play in organized club leagues, others play in leagues at public facilities that are open to all.

Indeed, tennis everyone.

What tennis enthusiasts everywhere love about tennis is its fierce competition, marvelous aerobic activity, and great mental stimulation. As a player becomes more proficient at hitting the ball over the net and into the court, tennis evolves into a game of quick bursts of action followed by relatively tranquil intervals.

The best thing I can say about tennis is that you'll never get bored playing it. It's a game that can be played by those ages six to eighty-six, which is why tennis is often promoted as a "sport of a lifetime." Another telling feature about tennis is that no matter what your level of ability, you see improvement every time you step on the court.

TENNIS MY WAY

Tennis has certainly been good to me, giving me twenty-two years on the women's professional tour before I retired in 1996. I saw the world, met fascinating people, made a nice living, and tried to be a light to other people.

From all my years of practicing and playing tennis, I have noticed that the game parallels our Christian life. The more you play tennis, the better you get, just as the more we pray and read the Bible, the more spiritually mature we become. I've long felt that the first game of each set creates the tone for the rest of the match. In a similar fashion, how we start the day often sets the tone for how the rest of the day will go. I know that my day goes better when I've read my Bible and spent time in God's Word, which gives me a foundation for dealing with the ups and downs of daily living.

On the tennis court, players use their groundstrokes — forehands and backhands — to probe for weaknesses in their opponents. Similarly, Satan probes for weaknesses in our lives, moving us around the court of life by serving up various temptations that can cause us to sin: jealousy, envy, pride, lust, alcohol, drugs, and sexual temptation, to name a few. How we handle those temptations determines whether we are victorious in the end.

There are some important differences, however, between tennis and the spiritual life. For instance, not just anyone can enter the U.S. Open or Wimbledon. You have to qualify by having a world ranking high enough to get "straight in" or by winning matches in a qualifying tournament. By contrast, we don't have to qualify to enter the kingdom of heaven. We've been accepted automatically into the draw by virtue of one thing: believing that Jesus Christ is the Son of God who died for our sins and paid the penalty for us on the Cross.

Lessons like these make me confident you're going to enjoy this book. It's been said that going through life without God is like playing tennis with the net down. I have to agree. Many of life's lessons have already taken place on the tennis court, which we can apply to our spiritual lives as well. All we need to do is play in His court.

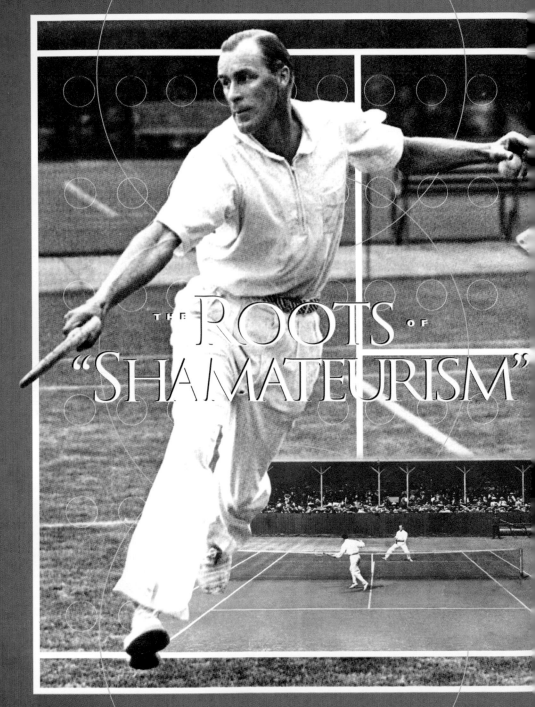

THE ROOTS OF "SHAMATEURISM"

In the game of tennis these days, some-one good enough — and fortunate enough — to win any of the four major world tennis tour-naments (the Australian Open, French Open, Wimbledon, and the U.S. Open) pockets a winner's check of around $800,000. That's pretty ho-hum news these days for the players and the sporting public — just another payday for multimillionaires. Pass the sugar, please.

Today's stars exhibit a certain indiffer-ence to all the dollars, marks, francs, pounds, and guilders tossed their way. As a former player who benefited from that largesse, I have to admit that it's a bit surrealistic to be paid such fantastic sums for playing such a pleasur-able game. The oversized check placards that winners hold up seem like Monopoly money.

It wasn't always that way. Prize money is

a fairly recent phenomenon in tennis' storied history, a history that is worth recounting.

A few thousand years ago tennis got its start when a couple of guys made a ball out of cloth layers and began batting it back and forth with their hands. Archaeologists have traced tennis to a Persian civilization of the fifth century B.C., although most tennis historians agree that French nobility began playing *jeu de paume* ("game of the palm") in the thirteenth century. That game became so popular that the Archbishop of Rouen banned priests from playing *jeu de paume* in 1245 because they were neglecting their pastoral duties.

In the Middle Ages, *jeu de paume* caught on with British royalty and wealthy landholders, who began calling this Gallic game "tennis," a play on the French word *tenez* (which means "to hold" or "to keep"). The modern game of tennis was invented by British Major Walter Clopton Wingfield in 1873 when he decided to liven up a garden party by introducing "lawn tennis" to his guests. Players knocked a plain rubber ball back and forth with wooden rackets strung with sheep intestines, not "catgut." The net was four feet high — a foot higher than today's net — and the court was shaped like an hourglass (narrow at the net, wider at the baseline).

Major Wingfield's guests had such a jolly good time that they began playing tennis in *their* aristocratic gardens. Today, you would hardly recognize the brand of tennis they played 125 years ago. Male opponents dwelled in the backcourt and patted the ball gently back and forth over the net. The idea was to not exert oneself to the point of breaking a sweat, lest perspiration soil the white, starched, long-sleeved shirt underneath the blue blazer. A thin necktie and white flannel trousers completed the sporting outfit.

When women played tennis, they donned flowing dresses and trussed themselves in cinched-tight corsets, making sure they wore several slips to guard against an untoward glimpse of an exposed ankle. Women, too, were expected to keep their movements genteel. Any sudden moves or running could prompt perspiration forming underneath their wide-brimmed hats with diaphanous veils — an unladylike proposition, to be sure.

The game became more athletic as man's competitive nature eventually won out. Human nature being what it is, the players wanted to know who was "king of the hill," so tennis' first tournament began on July 10, 1877, at Wimbledon. The drawsheet was filled with an undemocratic lot from Britain's upper-crust society who could afford to play and had access to courts in the backyards of gentry estates.

It didn't take long for tennis to catch on with the well-heeled on this side of the Atlantic. The United States Lawn Tennis Association, or USLTA, formed in 1881 as the sport's governing body in this country. The USLTA brought order to a sport that had different scoring systems, balls of differing sizes and weights, and courts with various dimensions.

Those controlling the game in modern tennis' first fifty years, however, also enacted policies that raised the bar very high and included only those white people who were rich enough to play the game. Further, the foundation was laid for a system in which players were not allowed to earn money playing or teaching tennis if they wanted to continue playing in "amateur" tennis tournaments.

In his book, *Tennis: A Game of Motion,* Eugene Scott writes, "The USLTA, in its early efforts to maintain order, retarded the game's progress by failing to assist and coordinate the growth of professional tennis." He continues, "Pro tennis, from the time of the first tour promoted by Charles C. ('Cash and Carry') Pyle in 1926, was considered an outlaw activity and was excommunicated by the USLTA. When the great players of the 1930s and 1940s — Bill Tilden, Fred Perry, Ellsworth Vines, Bobby Riggs, Don Budge and Jack Kramer — turned pro, the USLTA looked away with an attitude of 'That's not tennis, it doesn't concern us.' "

This institutional attitude gave way to an unofficial policy of "shamateurism," in which top players received modest payments for "expenses" (although most players received free food and lodging anyway) plus round-trip airfare. Jack Kramer, one of the game's great players from the late 1940s and 1950s, confessed in an article written in a Sunday supplement: "I was a paid amateur." He padded expense accounts like an unscrupulous business traveler, accepted hush payments from tournament directors, and toured the world with somebody else picking up the tab.

By the 1960s, something was rotten in Denmark and anywhere else "amateur" tennis was contested. "I played under the worst of the old shamateurism days," said Dennis Ralston, the No. 1-ranked U.S. player in the first half of that decade. "The hypocrisy of the USLTA was scary because they told us when we could play and where we could play."

The amateur system forced people with consciences to turn professional. "I was tired of taking dirty money," said Barry MacKay, one of my broadcast partners who turned pro in the mid-'60s. Tennis fans were equally tired of sham competition, since the sport's best players were banned from the biggest tournaments.

Although it took more than forty years, shamateurism eventually imploded when the British Lawn Tennis Association voted on December 14, 1967, to conduct the 1968 Wimbledon tournament as an "open" championship — open to professionals and amateurs. The rest of the tennis world quickly fell in line, and it was about time! Baseball had been paying players for one hundred years. Professional golf got its start during the Victorian Era of the 1890s. Professional football could trace its roots back to the 1920s, and the National Basketball Association to the late 1940s.

To me, there's a biblical principle at work here: Those who work deserve their pay, including spiritual "professionals," pastors, and church leaders. First Timothy 5 reminds us that faithful church leaders should receive enough financial support so that they will be able to provide for their families without unnecessary worry. We need to support pastors who lead and teach us. After all, who wants an "amateur" in the pulpit?

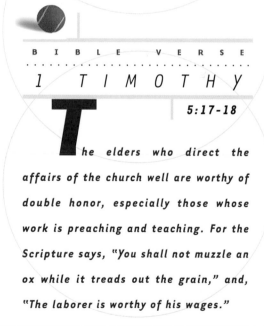

B I B L E   V E R S E

1 TIMOTHY

5:17-18

The elders who direct the affairs of the church well are worthy of double honor, especially those whose work is preaching and teaching. For the Scripture says, "You shall not muzzle an ox while it treads out the grain," and, "The laborer is worthy of his wages."

THE AGASSI AND THE ECSTACY

Andre Agassi fired a smoking first serve to Russian player Andrei Medvedev and watched the return sail long. As the capacity crowd erupted, Andre dropped his racket as if it were on fire. He turned and faced his coach, Brad Gilbert, in the player's box and cupped his unshaven face with his hands. His eyes watered and his mouth hung open in a mixture of joy and relief that signaled the unthinkable had happened: Andre Agassi had captured the 1999 French Open!

Ah, but it was more than that. At the ripe old age of twenty-nine, a time when everyone in tennis had written him off, Andre had just become the first man in thirty years to complete a career Grand Slam with the most improbable of comebacks, winning the final three sets against a determined opponent.

In the announcer's booth, NBC's John McEnroe surveyed the tumultuous scene at Roland Garros. "I'm speechless," said Mighty Mac, and that was saying something.

Andre blinked away tears as he approached the net to shake Medvedev's hand. When his vanquished opponent crossed over to Andre's side of the court to hug him, the tears turned into a flood.

Andre was overcome by his accomplishment, and who could blame him? He had become the first man to win a career Grand Slam on four different surfaces: the grass of Wimbledon (1992), the hardcourts of the U.S. Open (1994), the Rebound Ace of the Australian Open (1995), and now the red clay of Roland Garros. Back in 1969, when Rod Laver won the Grand Slam, three of the titles came on grass courts: the fourth was Paris' *terre batue.*

Andre's victory came after his game had slipped — make that *disappeared* — into a tennis black hole. His confidence shot, his skills eroded, and his body out-of-shape, Andre's ranking embarked on a free fall that took him from a world ranking of No. 1 in 1995 to No. 141 by 1997. After winning in Paris, reaching the Wimbledon finals, and winning the U.S. Open during that same summer of 1999, he reclaimed the No. 1 ranking.

Andre's story reminds me of a remarkable comeback in the Bible: a guy named Samson. Samson's account is told in the Old Testament's Book of Judges, at a time when God had delivered the Israelites into the hands of their enemies, the Philistines. A man named Manoah had a wife who was barren, yet an angel of the Lord told her that she would conceive and give birth to a special son, Samson, who would rescue Israel from the Philistines. The mother was given strict instructions to

never cut her son's hair.

Samson grew up with enormous physical strength, and his feats became legendary. He tore apart a lion. Killed thirty men in Ashkelon. Caught three hundred foxes, tied their tails together in pairs, then torched the tails and let the foxes run through the Philistine fields, burning their grain and olive trees. Samson even slaughtered one thousand Philistines with a donkey's jawbone.

News of Samson's enormous physical strength swept through the land, but it turned out that he was no match for the weaker sex. He was seduced by a Philistine woman named Delilah, who eventually betrayed the secret of his strength to the enemy: if Samson got a haircut, his strength would leave him.

While Samson was sleeping, the Philistines cut his hair, then captured him, gouged his eyes out, and tossed him into a dungeon to rot. Samson became a shell of his former glory. Soon, the Philistine leaders decided to make a little sport at Samson's expense by bringing him out to Centre Court where the people gloated and hurled abuse and rotten tomatoes his way.

Samson outwardly took the abuse while inwardly forming a plan: he would play his final match and go out as a winner for God. He prayed, "O Lord God remember me, I pray! Strengthen me, I pray, just this once, O God, that I may with one blow take vengeance on the Philistines for my two eyes!" (Judg. 16:28).

Straddling two pillars, the chained, blind Samson pushed with God-given strength and sent the stadium crashing down, killing all in attendance. Samson's comeback was complete. He achieved a great victory for Israel, paid with his life and received his applause on the eternal Centre Court.

BIBLE VERSE

JUDGES 16:29-30

And Samson took hold of the two middle pillars which supported the temple, and he braced himself against them, one on his right and the other on his left. Then Samson said, "Let me die with the Philistines!" And he pushed with all his might, and the temple fell on the lords and all the people who were in it. So the dead that he killed at his death were more than he had killed in his life.

THE MOTHER'S DAY MASSACRE

CHAPTER

Statistically, Margaret Court might have been the greatest person who ever played the game of tennis. She won twenty-four of the "major" tournaments and captured the Grand Slam in 1970. (The Grand Slam is winning the Australian, French, Wimbledon, and U.S. Open in the same calendar year. Only Margaret, Maureen Connolly, and Steffi Graf have accomplished this feat on the women's side.)

Winning twenty-four major singles titles is a record that still stands. Steffi Graf came up short with twenty-two. But no one — male or female — is within shouting distance of Margaret's record sixty-two Grand Slam championships in singles, doubles, and mixed doubles.

Since many of those victories came

before tennis opened the game to professional players in 1968 and now competition is much more fierce, it's unlikely that her record will ever be broken. The tennis world pays scant attention to the legacy of this great player, however, not only because she's chosen to live outside the public eye but also because of her outspoken faith.

When Margaret Court returned to Wimbledon during the 2000 Championships for the Parade of Champions, she returned to Centre Court's pampered grass as the Rev. Margaret Court. Margaret became an ordained minister in 1991, and today she is senior pastor of Margaret Court Ministries, an international organization based on the non-denominational Victory of Life Centre, which she founded in her hometown of Perth, Australia.

Her faith wasn't always so evident. Margaret was a sidelines Christian until 1972 when she stayed with some friends in the United States who kept thrusting "little books" into her hands. Most of the books were tossed out, but she kept one that explained the Gospel and instructed the reader how to accept Christ into his or her life. Intrigued, she began attending church meetings. Not long after, she gave her heart to Christ.

Margaret was thirty then, with five years of professional tennis left before retiring in 1977 when she was pregnant with her third child. While not everyone in tennis remembers Margaret, Margaret certainly remembers a certain match in 1973 when she agreed to play fifty-five-year-old Bobby Riggs in a "Battle of the Sexes" match.

Bobby, a duck-walking, bespectacled player, was the world's No. 1 player in 1939, and he liked to hustle people. In other words, he liked to separate people from their money by winning bets. In the early

1970s, women's professional tennis was in its infancy. Billie Jean King and the leading players had banded together to form the Virginia Slims tour, but crowds and press attention were slim.

Bobby began boasting to anyone who would listen that he — an over-the-hill, geriatric player in his mid-fifties — could still beat the top female professionals. Before she knew it, Margaret was staring across the net at Bobby Riggs with a national television audience looking on. Bobby made good on his boasts and bets as he hustled Margaret off the court, 6-2, 6-1. The press called it the "Mother's Day Massacre."

I never had a chance to talk to Margaret about it, but her shellacking didn't turn out to be a bad thing for women's tennis. Billie Jean King stepped up to defend women's tennis' honor and challenged Riggs to a *mano-a-mano* showdown. That's what Bobby was hoping for, and on September 20, 1973, more than thirty thousand spectators in the Houston Astrodome and a television audience of fifty million watched one of the most-talked-about events in American sports.

Billie Jean made Bobby look like an old man, winning handily. With help from the overwhelming publicity surrounding the match, women's tennis took off weeks before I turned eighteen in 1974, the year I decided to turn pro. We had a chance to play a unified tour instead of one divided by two organizations. That was also the year that Title IX mandated scholarships for women's collegiate athletics.

I can make the case that God used the "Mother's Day Massacre" for good. I'm sure that Margaret would have preferred to have won that match, but her loss shows that God can use anything, even an embarrassing defeat. Margaret, to her credit, became a forerunner in women's tennis and God's kingdom. In the Bible, there are many

examples of other forerunners: Moses for Joshua, David for Solomon, and John the Baptist for Jesus.

Thanks, Margaret, for preparing the way.

M A T T H E W

13:1-3

In those days John the Baptist came preaching in the wilderness of Judea, and saying, "Repent, for the kingdom of heaven is at hand!" For this is he who was spoken of by the prophet Isaiah, saying: "The voice of one crying in the wilderness: 'Prepare the way of the Lord; make His paths straight.' "

Arthur Ashe was tennis' Jackie Robinson, the first African-American male player to rise to the top of the tennis world in 1975. (On the women's side, pioneer status belongs to Althea Gibson, who won Wimbledon and the U.S. Open twice in the late 1950s.)

Arthur grew up in segregated Richmond, Virginia, where Negroes were relegated to the back of the bus and to "black only" drinking fountains. His aunt, Dorothy Brown, recalls the time that Arthur, who couldn't have been more than six or seven years old, boarded a crowded bus with his mother. Arthur approached a white man and politely asked whether he would give up his seat for his mother. The man thought for a minute.

POETRY IN GRACE

"Normally I don't give my seat for black people, but I like your grit," said the fellow. "She can have my seat."

That anecdote sums up much of Arthur's life. He was exceedingly polite — but not deferential — in a white man's sport, and he had a knack for opening doors for racial equality. His greatest legacy is probably his trips to South Africa in the 1970s, where he quietly demanded to play before "mixed" audiences in a country that practiced apartheid.

His greatest on-court victories were winning Wimbledon and tennis' first "open" U.S. Open in 1968 as an amateur. At that time, Arthur collected a loving cup and $28 a day in expense money, while his vanquished foe, Tom Okker, a professional from the Netherlands, banked the $14,000 top prize money for being the runner-up. Arthur eventually turned pro, and his memorable triumph over Jimmy Connors at Wimbledon in 1975 is considered one of the greatest upsets of all time. Very few had guessed Arthur stood a chance against Connors, but Arthur had beaten the odds all his life.

That changed however, when Arthur suffered a heart attack at age thirty-six, an event that made national news. He never played competitive tennis again. Four years later, Arthur submitted to double-bypass heart surgery, during which he received a blood transfusion. A new disease was making the news — the media called it AIDS — but blood testing for the HIV virus was not in place at the time.

Five years passed. While undergoing routine tests in conjunction with brain surgery, Arthur received stunning news: he was HIV-positive, due to tainted donor blood used in that transfusion. His wife Jeanne and daughter Camera were tested. Fortunately, their results were negative. But in those days, an HIV diagnosis was tantamount to a death sentence — and carried a social stigma.

Arthur kept the news a secret for several years because he didn't want anyone to feel sorry for him. When faced with the possibility of *USA Today* breaking the story in 1992, however, Arthur called a news conference to announce his battle with AIDS. He accepted his fate with dignity and class, knowing that he didn't have long to live. Arthur died less than a year later at the age of forty-nine.

The Bible teaches us that it is appointed unto man once to die. We don't know the day or the hour that we will meet God in all his glory. I don't know where Arthur stood spiritually as he stood on the precipice of eternity. Almost two decades earlier, he wrote about his lagging faith in his 1973 book, *Arthur Ashe: Portrait in Motion*. After he attended his grandmother's funeral at Westwood Baptist Church in Richmond, he says, "I never let on to Big Mama [his grandmother] that I had stopped believing in Jesus. I always kept on going to Sunday school and acting in all the church plays. I guess most of my family still assumes that I am a Christian, but I've always been very skeptical."

Did he have a change of heart while he lay on his deathbed? I hope so. What about you? What will others say about your faith? Will they say it was as solid as a concrete tennis backboard, or will people just "assume" that you are a Christian?

We don't know how much time we have on this earth. The time to think about your spiritual future is now, when you can do something about it. I can state one thing with certainty: those two Grand Slam trophies aren't worth very much to Arthur now. Our goal in life is to have eternal crowns laid up for us in heaven. Our prized everlasting trophy is knowing Jesus Christ as our personal savior and Lord of our life.

BIBLE VERSE

PHILIPPIANS

3:14

I press toward the goal for the **prize of the upward call of God in Christ Jesus.**

WE ALL
TIGHTEN UP

Jana Novotna tugged at her headband and fidgeted with her skirt while she prepared to serve at the cathedral of tennis, Wimbledon's famed Centre Court. With a huge lead in the third set against Steffi Graf, Jana stood just five points from the greatest victory in her tennis life. She didn't have far to go, and she knew it.

For the last set and a half, Jana had been cleaning Steffi's clock with brilliant forays to the net that ended with angle volleys for winners. The scoreboard showed her leading 6-7, 6-1, 4-1 and 40-30. One more point and the score would be 5-1, with two chances to serve for the most coveted title in tennis.

On the 40-30 point, however, Jana doublefaulted. Not to worry. The game was still deuce. When Steffi didn't strike the service return cleanly, however, the ball sat up for Jana to put away with a forehand volley. She charged the net with her racket ready to knock the "sitter" for a crosscourt winner. It was supposed to be a routine shot, one that Jana had practiced ten thousand times and could make 99 percent of the time.

On this occasion, however, she overhit so badly that the ball nearly landed in the Royal Box! In tennis talk, Jana "got the elbow." Choked under pressure. And now she was in trouble. With the chair umpire announcing "Advantage Graf" and the crowd clapping in anticipation, Jana must have been kicking herself over how badly she played that pressure-packed forehand volley.

When you blow a big shot, you're supposed to slow things down, take a deep breath, and remind yourself that there's still plenty of tennis to be played. All players choke at one time or another; there isn't a player alive who hasn't missed an easy shot when it counted most. Instead of righting the ship, however, Jana began taking on more water. At the end of a long, contested point, an overhead into the net conceded the game to Steffi.

Suddenly, the body language of both players reversed. Now it was Steffi who had more spring to her step, while Jana slumped her shoulders and picked at her racket strings as she walked over to the deuce court to return Steffi's serve.

Jana fought back, taking Steffi to 15-40 at 2-4, but Steffi saved two break points with an ace and a forehand volley error from Jana. At 4-3, Jana suffered a total meltdown before a worldwide audience. A doublefault at 30-30. A saved break point, then another doublefault at deuce, followed by yet another doublefault.

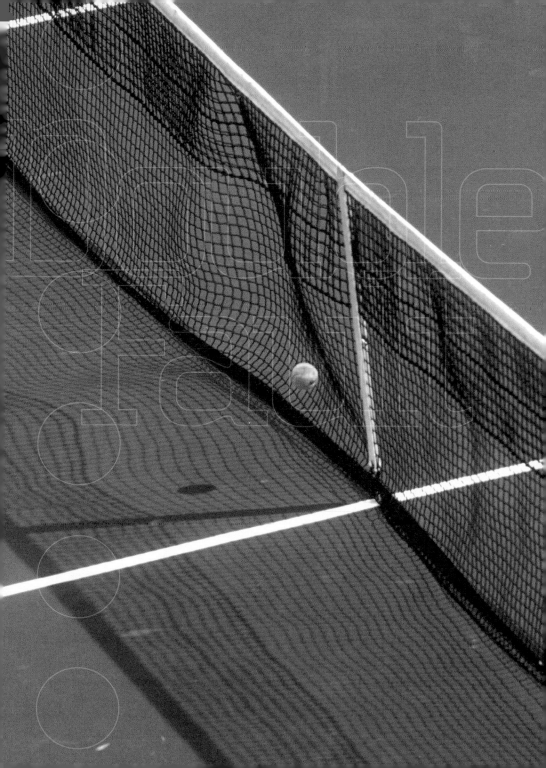

It was painful to watch such a valiant effort dissipate in a flurry of missed service returns, ill-timed volleys, and shocking doublefaults. Jana would never win another game. Probably the only person who didn't feel sorry for her was Steffi, who readily accepted the final five games and the third set, 6-4, to claim her fifth Wimbledon crown.

Jana shook Steffi's hand, bussed her on the cheek, and slumped in her chair while Wimbledon officials prepared for the on-court presentation of the trophies. Ever since she was a little girl growing up in Brno, Czechoslovakia, Jana had dreamed of the day when the Duchess of Kent would hand her the winner's plate, which she would lift high above her head as the flashbulbs popped.

Instead, the Duchess of Kent shook Jana's hand as she presented her with the much smaller runner-up plate. That's when Jana lost it. She crumpled like a schoolgirl into the Duchess' arms, then rested her head on the royal's shoulder and wept.

We're told, too, that on the eve of the Crucifixion, the apostle Peter wept bitterly after denying three times that he knew Jesus. Peter, one of the Twelve — the "rock" upon whom the Lord would build his church — choked when asked whether he knew the Savior.

"I don't know what you're talking about," he said when a servant girl said that she had seen him with Jesus of Galilee. Three times, Peter blew his chance to stand up for Jesus, just as Christ had predicted.

We all "tighten up" sometimes when it comes to standing up for the Lord. What will you say if someone at work asks:

• "Hey, you go to church, don't you?"
• "You're not one of those people who call themselves Christians, are you?"

• "You're not one those religious fanatics who doesn't believe in a woman's right to choose, are you?"

Are you mentally prepared to defend your faith? To stand up for Jesus? To articulate your beliefs on the moral issues of the day?

Even if you blow it, you'll probably get a second chance. Jana Novotna did, and she made the most of hers in the 1998 Wimbledon final when she overcame her jittery nerves to defeat Nathalie Tauziat 6-4, 7-6. This time, the Duchess of Kent took both of Jana's hands and said, "I'm so proud of you."

Won't it be great if Jesus someday says the same thing to us?

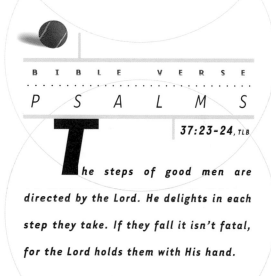

BIBLE VERSE

PSALMS

37:23-24, TLB

The steps of good men are directed by the Lord. He delights in each step they take. If they fall it isn't fatal, for the Lord holds them with His hand.

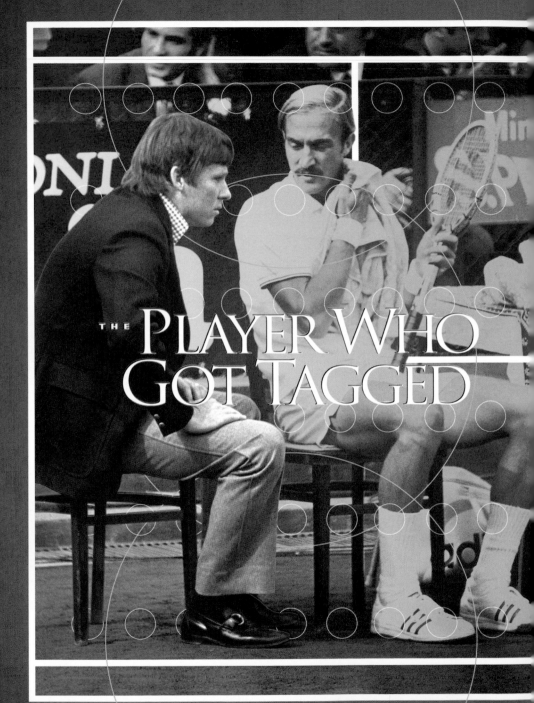

THE PLAYER WHO GOT TAGGED

When Dennis Ralston was nine years old, his parents put him on a bus from Bakersfield, California, to Los Angeles, where he was to compete in a junior tournament at the Los Angeles Tennis Club. It seems incomprehensible that any right-minded parents would put their third-grade son on a Greyhound bus bound for Los Angeles, but this was 1951, a time far more innocent than today.

Dennis remembers being dropped off at the intersection of Hollywood and Vine and catching a local bus to the L.A. Tennis Club. The youngster had been prepared for this moment. His father had given him a cut-down wooden racket just after he learned to walk, and the young boy loved nothing better than beating an old ball against a brick wall in the back of the house. When he appeared at the L.A. Tennis Club with racket and valise in hand, he looked up at Perry Jones, the dictatorial head of the Southern California Tennis Association, and said, "I'm Dennis."

"Dennis, who?" replied Perry Jones.

"Why, I'm Dennis Ralston. Where do I stay?" the precocious youngster replied.

From that day forward, Dennis was in the game. He became an accomplished player in the 1960s during the last days of tennis' amateurs-only era and has followed those early days with a successful coaching career, most notably as Chris Evert's coach. But there's something more you should know about Dennis.

A month after graduating from high school, Dennis astounded the tennis world by capturing the Wimbledon men's doubles championship with Rafael Osuna of Mexico. He was just seventeen years old, and many more championships were predicted for this young upstart.

Dennis was a determined young man who fought for every point. He didn't go for this "gentlemanly" tennis often expressed in the journals of the day. He scraped and hustled, relying on heavily muscled legs and powerful shoulders to overpower and outplay his opponents.

He was his own worst critic. Whenever Dennis missed an easy

shot or hit wide on a passing shot, he chastised himself for the error. Such remonstrations weren't heard of in those days. It was keeping a "stiff upper lip" that showed you were a "jolly good sport."

Because of his outbursts, the press turned on him.

"He seems, at times, to be a man firmly arrayed against himself," wrote scribe Jack Olsen. "It is not only that he has a bad temper, but he repeatedly has been in trouble for disturbing domestic and international tranquility by throwing his racket and making menacing gestures at the crowd. What manner of ruffian is this?" Olsen wrote, even though Dennis had never actually thrown his racket.

Another tennis journalist, in a moment of inspiration, called him "Dennis the Menace," no doubt because Hank Ketchum's cartoon strip had become very popular, spawning a TV sitcom in the early '60s.

"Dennis rhymed with menace, so I got tagged," Dennis told me. "I was the No. 1 U.S. player, and while I wasn't a saint out there, by today's comparison, I was an angel."

In 1962, Dennis was playing a pivotal Davis Cup doubles match in Cleveland. Dennis and partner Chuck McKinley were locked in a duel with Tony Palafox and Mexico's Rafael Osuna, Dennis' roommate at the University of Southern California and doubles partner in the Grand Slam events. Late in the third set, with set point for the Americans,

McKinley served to Osuna. Just as the Mexican started his return, Dennis faked a poaching move, but he slipped and fell flat on his face in the red clay. If Dennis had been able to hold his ground, he easily would have been able to put away Osuna's weak return. Instead, all he could do was watch Rafael's dead-quail shot pass by tantalizingly within reach.

Dennis swore — not at the Mexicans, but at himself. He was frustrated that he had lost his footing, ticked off that his shirt and shorts were caked in red clay, and boiling mad that his team had squandered a set point. He fumed for several minutes. After the Americans lost the match in five sets, tennis writers cut Dennis to shreds.

Reports from Cleveland detailed how an angry Ralston had cursed spectators and players alike, refused a towel from a Mexican coach, and generally acted like an ugly American. From then on, Dennis was a marked man. The press kept up the "Dennis the Menace" drumbeat until the U.S. Lawn Tennis Association, the governing body at the time, suspended Dennis from playing tournaments for the rest of the year — all because he got mad at himself.

Dennis became a Christian in 1972, shortly after the U.S. Davis Cup win in Bucharest. His faith is now as rock-solid as his forehand volley used to be, but there are still people who associate him with his bad-boy days.

Have you ever been tagged by others? Does your past haunt you? When Christ comes into our lives, we become new creations. Fortunately, He forgets our pasts — all the blunders, all the mistakes, all the disobedience, and all the sins. We don't have to live in the past, which is great news for all of us. All we have to do is ask forgiveness for our past mistakes; God is quick to forgive. In fact, Psalm 103:12 says that God forgives our sins as far as the east is from the west, and He doesn't remember them anymore. Furthermore, 2 Corinthians 5:17 says, "Therefore, if anyone is in Christ, he is a new creation; old things have passed away; behold, all things have become new."

That's good news to Dennis — and to you and me, too!

BIBLE VERSE

HEBREWS

8:12

For I will be merciful to their unrighteousness, and their sins and their lawless deeds I will remember no more.

FAST THINGS CHANGE

In the fall of 1989, I flew to Moscow for the first-ever Virginia Slims' professional tennis tournament. That week, major upheavals were taking place around the world. An earthquake interrupted the "Bay Series" between the San Francisco Giants and the Oakland A's, and Mikhail Gorbachev and his *glasnost* policy of openness shook up the political landscape, opening up the Soviet Union to new things — including women's professional tennis. None of us knew that more dramatic political changes were waiting around the corner. Just one month later, the Berlin Wall separating East Germany and West Germany fell, creating dramatic changes in Eastern bloc countries.

I was nearing the end of my playing career, so I eagerly signed up to play the new

Deuce

Moscow event because I had never been to the Soviet Union. Since this was shaping up to be a once-in-a-lifetime chance, I asked my mother, Marty Newcomer; my sister, Jody Jones; and my coach, Paul Wilkens, to join me.

I'll never forget the eve of my first-round match. The four of us walked from our hotel to Red Square. Under the dramatic nighttime lighting, we pretended to march like Russian soldiers. The guards who glared in suspicion were neither amused nor particularly cooperative when we asked to take photos of them.

I drew an unusual 9 a.m. start for my opening match at the Olympic indoor tennis stadium. On the ride over to the venue, the four of us bunched up in a chauffeur-driven minibus.

"You know, you look good, Paul," my mother commented to my coach. "I don't think I've ever seen you look so well."

"Thanks," Paul said, as he continued to take in the sights. I shot a glance at Paul, a fifty-four-year-old teaching pro with a chipper attitude and a perpetual tan. His skin looked smooth, as if the crisp Russian air had been an elixir for middle-age wrinkles.

I had arranged to warm up with Larissa Neiland, a top Russian player, prior to the match. Upon arrival, Larissa wasn't anywhere to be seen, so Paul grabbed a racket to rally with me. He began spraying balls all over the place, which frustrated me since I was trying to find my rhythm before my match. He seemed out of sorts, but then a few minutes later, Larissa showed up to practice with me.

Paul took his place at the net and watched us loosen up. He popped open a pressurized can of balls; the *pssst* caused me to glance in his direction. That's when I saw Paul keel over and fall face down on the court, spread-eagled like a crime victim. For an instant, I thought it was another joke about the KGB, but when Paul failed to move, I became very concerned. Mom sprinted over and reached him first. She turned him over, and his eyes were open, staring into space. Mom immediately began CPR and mouth-to-mouth resuscitation while I ran for help.

Assistance was hard to find that early in the morning. (They didn't have 911 in Russia). By the time paramedics arrived a half hour later, Paul was gone, having breathed his last on a Russian tennis court. I later learned that his smooth skin that morning was a sign of fluids building up in his body.

I had never seen anyone die at my feet before. I looked at Paul's face, frozen in time. He had planned to be married the following week in Paris — a new start in life. Instead, his existence on earth was over.

The tournament director postponed my match to that night, and we went to retrieve Paul's belongings back at the hotel. We found an address book and began making calls. At 9 p.m., I played my match and lost. My heart just wasn't in it.

The memory of that day is always a reminder to me that we know not the day nor the hour when we will come into glory — and judgment — before the Lord Jesus Christ. One of the most oft-quoted clichés is the one about "living one day at a time." The fact remains, however, that each day we live takes us one day closer to that final day.

That point was driven home again one Sunday when I heard my mom's pastor, Richard Ollinger, ask, "What would you do if you knew that you had only a year to live?" He then gave me some words of advice:

1. Make sure your most important relationship — the one with God — is right.

2. Uphold your responsibilities with honor. Keep short accounts. Don't run up the credit cards.

3. Confirm your relationships with your spouse, children, and family members. Talk to them and your friends as if you had already passed away and you wish you hadn't left something unsaid. Live your remaining time without regrets.

I've tried to take Pastor Ollinger's advice to heart, but like all of us, it's difficult to live as though you had only a short time left. I try to start each day in prayer and Bible reading, asking God to direct me according to His perfect will. I try to treat others as I would want them to treat me. I strive to confirm my relationships with those I love and those who are close to me. If I keep my eyes on these things, I can rest assured that whatever each day holds for me, I am in His hands.

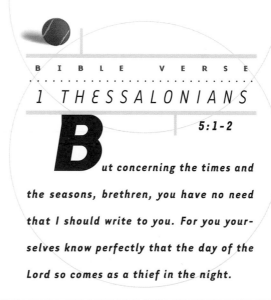

BIBLE VERSE

1 THESSALONIANS

5:1-2

But concerning the times and the seasons, brethren, you have no need that I should write to you. For you yourselves know perfectly that the day of the Lord so comes as a thief in the night.

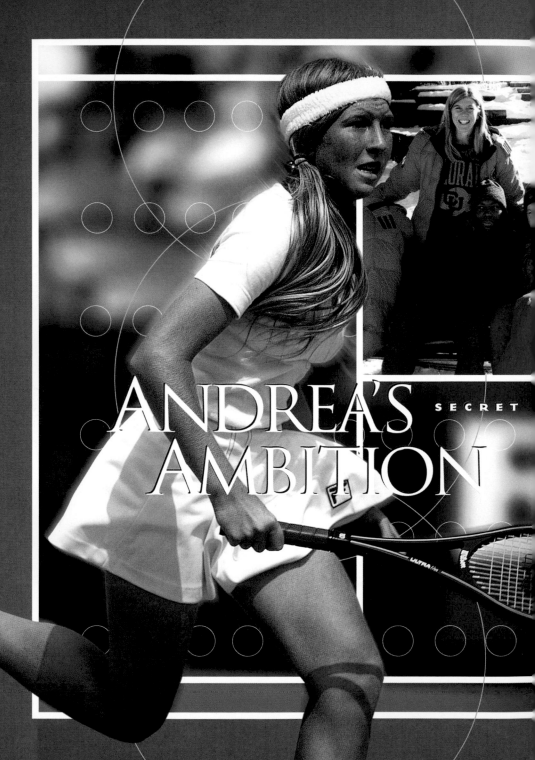

ANDREA'S
AMBITION

SECRET

The women's locker room can be a cruel place, especially when you're fourteen years old, still wearing pigtails and braces, still waiting for your body to get through puberty. It doesn't help when you're also challenging the world's best players for a piece of the prize money pie and you're just a 5'4", 118-pound high school freshman from Lincolnshire, Illinois — and a confident one at that.

That was what Andrea Jaeger's life was like back in 1979. Many of my fellow pros shunned her like a Jehovah's Witness at the front door whenever she stepped into the locker room. Once she passed out of earshot, they gave her the Cruella DeVil routine. Things got so bad that Andrea started dressing in the public restroom before her matches. This led to the bizarre scene of fans following Andrea into the women's bathroom, slipping magazines and photos underneath her stall, asking for her autograph.

Too young to fit into the professional tennis world and too famous to make friends back at Adlai Stevenson High School, Andrea struggled mostly alone. Driven hard by her father and coach, Roland, a tough guy who was a former professional boxer, Andrea retreated further into her shell.

A couple of years later during the U.S. Open, Andrea decided to do some window shopping in Manhattan. She stopped and looked at a toy store's window display of games, stuffed animals, and puzzles. She had plenty of money to buy anything she saw, but no time to play with any of those toys. Her childhood had been spent on a tennis court. Then the thought occurred to her. *What about the kids who have the time to play with toys but no money to purchase them?* An idea slowly took root. *Why not buy some toys and present them to some kids who would really appreciate them?*

She located a nearby hospital with a children's cancer ward, then purchased hundreds of dollars of toys, stuffed animals, and hand-held games. She visited the oncology ward where children the same age as she — and some years younger — were staring death straight in the face. She passed out gifts, worked on puzzles, and goofed around with the cancer-stricken kids. No one knew who Andrea Jaeger was, and no one cared. No publicists or camera crews followed her.

Andrea liked it that way. The impact of bringing a small measure of joy to youngsters fighting to reach their next birthday transformed the teen tennis star. She began visiting cancer wards at every tour stop, and *no one knew who she was!* Eventually, some people figured it out, but none of us in the locker room knew about Andrea's secret ambition.

Meanwhile, Andrea's world ranking soared to No. 2. She reached two Grand Slam finals, then blew out her shoulder at the 1984 French Open and was never the same player again. Four years after that, a drunk driver smashed into her Volkswagen, fracturing two vertebrae and aborting her comeback.

Fortunately, Andrea had saved much of her prize winnings (estimated at $1.3 million), and as she took stock of her future, she decided that she felt fulfilled when working with gravely ill children. She started small by publishing an upbeat newsletter for the kids and taking calls on a special 800-number. I remember hearing stories of how Andrea spent hours on the phone talking with these terminally ill children, being a friend and even traveling to their homes. She gave freely of herself.

She founded a non-profit organization in the early 1990s called the Kids Stuff Foundation, basing it in Aspen, Colorado. She started a summer camp and began inviting kids to spend a week with her in the Rocky Mountains doing "normal" stuff like playing volleyball, making s'mores around the campfire, and going on day hikes.

The Kids Stuff Foundation is now the **Silver Lining Foundation** — a place where very sick children go for a very special adventure. What Andrea has accomplished underscores an important spiritual principle: that we should stop focusing on what's happening to us and reach out to help those less fortunate. This not only helps those who need it but also demonstrates to the world that we take seriously Jesus' charge to feed the hungry, provide shelter for the homeless,

1994
1995

1975. A.R.ASHE.
1976. B.BORG.
1977. B.BORG.
1978. B.BORG.
1979. B.BORG.
1980. B.BORG.
1981. J.P.McENROE.
1982. J.S.CONNORS.
1983. J.P.McENROE.
1984. J.P.McENROE.
1985. B.BECKER.
1986. B.BECKER.
1987. P.CASH.
1988. S.EDBERG.
1989. B.BECKER.
1990. S.EDBERG.
1991. M.STICH.
1992. A.AGASSI.
1993. P.SAMPRAS.

and visit the sick.

Like Andrea, I've also sought to take Jesus' words to heart. I volunteer my time with the **House of Hope**, a home for troubled teens in Orlando. The House of Hope has an astonishing 95 percent success rate in restoring rebellious, drug-ridden, cult-involved, sexually abused or hurting teenagers back to their families.

I conduct tennis clinics for the House of Hope teens, and I often invite them all — around fifty of them — over to our home for the day. We are fortunate to live on a lake and to have a pool and spa in our backyard. We let the kids water-ski and wake board on the lake, frolic in the pool, hit tennis balls on our tennis court — and then let them eat us out of house and home.

And that's just fine with me.

B I B L E   V E R S E

M A T T H E W

25:35-40

'For I was hungry and you gave Me food; I was thirsty and you gave Me drink; I was a stranger and you took Me in; I was naked and you clothed Me; I was sick and you visited Me; I was in prison and you came to Me.'

"Then the righteous will answer Him, saying, 'Lord, when did we see You hungry and feed You, or thirsty and give You drink? 'When did we see You a stranger and take You in, or naked and clothe You? 'Or when did we see You sick, or in prison, and come to You?'"

"And the King will answer and say to them, 'Assuredly, I say to you, inasmuch as you did it to one of the least of these My brethren, you did it to Me.'"

I consider my good friend Mary Carillo to be the best tennis commentator on the planet. She has a knack for capturing the nuances of what's happening on the court and coupling those insights with colorful phrases and descriptions. Topspin, in Maryspeak, is "putting work" on the ball, and players who find themselves down a set and two service breaks are said to be "toast."

Mary also coined the term "Big Babe" tennis while watching a bulked-up Mary Pierce bash groundstrokes off both wings on the way to her Australian Open victory several years ago. These days, the leading practitioners of "Big Babe" tennis are Lindsay Davenport, Venus and Serena Williams, and Mary Pierce. You could say that Anna Kournikova, the media darling who has a

CHAPTER 9

THE HEAVY HITTERS

stunning presence on and off the court, plays a lite version of the power game.

These talented young women are not interested in patiently working a point or moving their opponents out of position before throwing in a drop shot. Instead, they whack the ball from corner to corner, blast mid-court winners, and don't hold anything back on full-swing volleys. The Williams sisters clock their serves as hard and as fast as many male players.

"Big Babe" tennis is certainly fun to watch, which is why the women's game has never been more popular. Even John McEnroe, who disparaged women's tennis as "boring," has become a believer.

Similarly, we can find several "Big Babe" women in the Bible who were the heavy spiritual hitters of their day. I'm talking about Ruth, Naomi, Deborah, Esther, Rahab, and Mary. Let's look at how they match up.

Ruth and Naomi: This doubles pairing of mother-in-law and daughter-in-law eventually had an influence on the whole world. Ruth married Naomi's son, but after he died, Ruth became a destitute young widow. Naomi, also widowed, suggested that Ruth return to her family where her chances of finding a husband would be improved. Ruth wouldn't hear of it. She insisted on staying with Naomi and continued to shower her mother-in-law with kindness.

They traveled together to Bethlehem, confident that this was where God was leading them. Ruth's high moral character and willingness to work hard in the fields made her attractive to Boaz, a rich landowner. Naomi helped arrange Ruth's marriage to Boaz, even though it could weaken their relationship. However, Ruth did not allow her new marriage to change her loyalty to her former mother-in-law, and they both became

prosperous. God definitely had a plan for these gracious "Big Babes," as Ruth bore a son who became the grandfather of King David.

Deborah: The Bible records few women in national leadership positions, yet Deborah was tapped by God to become the only female Judge of Israel. We are told that she had wonderful leadership skills and deflected all praise to God. In a sense, she saw God as her on-court coach, and Deborah was willing to allow the Lord to lead her in bringing the people back to Him.

Esther: You could say that Esther was the Anna Kournikova of her day, a young Jewish woman whose beauty was so striking that the Persian King Ahasuerus took her as his queen. Esther used her favored position to approach King Ahasuerus on behalf of her people, but only after a "training period" of fasting and praying. Seeking an audience with the king was a bold gambit for Esther, who understood that she was risking her life. Esther informed King Ahasuerus that there was a plot against her people, the Jews. The king, because of his wife's plea, saved God's chosen people from destruction.

Rahab: Rahab was a prostitute inside the walled city of Jericho. She risked her life for a God she hardly knew, the Israelites' God, by hiding Israelite spies in her house of ill repute. She knew that if she was discovered by the local police, it would cost her the match.

Rahab accepted the risk of protecting the spies, proving that she was a player to be reckoned with. She eventually found God to be her partner on the court of life: when the walls fell down and Jericho was destroyed, her household was spared.

Mary: Like a young phenom winning a Grand Slam title before she is out of her teens, Mary secured her place in history when God tapped her to be the mother of the Son of God. Mary has a record that will never be broken: giving birth while remaining a virgin.

Mary is a reminder that God can involve ordinary people in extraordinary events, if only we make ourselves available to Him. Mary, never doubting how pregnancy would be possible, said, "Behold the maidservant of the Lord! Let it be to me according to your word" (Luke 1:38).

God placed each one of these "Big Babes" in the Bible to teach us about service, generosity, and a willingness to go to the extreme so that our lives can become more like Jesus.

Then we'll become His heavy hitters.

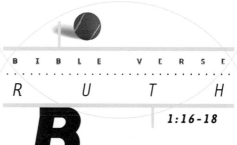

BIBLE VERSE
. . . .
R U T H

1:16-18

But Ruth said: "Entreat me not to leave you, or to turn back from following after you; for wherever you go, I will go; and wherever you lodge, I will lodge; your people shall be my people, and your God, my God. Where you die, I will die, and there will I be buried. The Lord do so to me, and more also, if anything but death parts you and me." When she saw that she was determined to go with her, she stopped speaking to her.*

A RITUAL HERE,
A RITUAL THERE

They're called "rituals" — little habits or movements that tennis players do over and over before the start of a point. Baseball has them, too. Before every pitch, some pitchers step off the mound, rub the ball with both hands, step back on the mound, sweep the rubber with their right foot, bend at the waist, look to the catcher for a sign, and then go into their windup. Meanwhile, batters go through their *own* set of rituals: tapping home plate with the end of their bats, rolling their shoulders, tapping the top of their helmets, taking several practice swings, and waggling their bats while they wait for the pitch.

Tennis players employ similar routines between points. Monica Seles always tugs at the bill of her cap with her right hand just before making her ball toss. Mary Joe Fernandez bounces the ball three times before serving into the deuce court and four times before serving in the ad court. Lindsay Davenport pulls at the top of her tennis shirt and wipes her brow between points. When John McEnroe was ready to serve, he tugged at the left shoulder of his shirt, patted his curls, then stooped over like the Hunchback of Notre Dame before making his ball toss.

Andre Agassi has his own set of serving rituals. While pacing about the backcourt, Andre asks the ballboy for three balls to be placed on his racket head while he wipes his brow with a towel. Then he hands the ballboy his towel, takes all three balls into his left hand and rotates them before tapping one back to the ballboy. He's probably looking for the lightest balls — the ones with the least nape on their covers — because they travel through the air faster. Andre is well aware that a serve just a few miles per hour faster could result in more service winners.

Ivan Lendl, the No. 1 player for several years in the 1980s, was probably No. 1 when it came to serving rituals. Each and every time he served — around two hundred times a match — he stepped up to the baseline and swept it with his left foot. Then Ivan reached into his right pocket and took a pinch of sawdust, which he applied and rubbed onto his racket grip. Next, he rotated the two balls in his left hand against his stomach before depositing one into his left pocket. Finally, Ivan reached up and either rubbed his eyebrows or plucked an eyebrow — ouch! After going through these machinations, Ivan was ready — and I'm sure that his opponent was mentally worn out.

That's probably why those who return serve often exercise their

own set of rituals. Many players pace around the backcourt like caged lions, or they turn to the ballboy and wave a hand in front of their faces, signaling that they would like a towel to wipe themselves off. Others, like Jimmy Connors and Andre Agassi, are famous for straightening their strings between points. Pete Sampras and Michael Chang sometimes use a small metal "string straightener" to adjust their string beds.

When it's time to play, many players skip in place while they wait to return serve, explaining why Spain's Arantxa Sanchez-Vicario is nicknamed "The Barcelona Bumblebee." Others bend at the waist or twirl their rackets like majorettes spinning their batons.

Some rituals border on the superstitious. Betty Stove, a Dutch player in the 1970s, refused to step on lines between points. She certainly looked awkward tiptoeing through a minefield of lines when the point was over.

I've had doubles partners who would only sit to the right of the chair umpire, or insisted on eating the same prematch meal repeatedly during a winning streak.

I never had any superstitions when I was playing, although I did have some rituals I followed. I always checked the shock absorber in my racket strings just before I served, which gave me time to clear my mind before making my ball toss. I found that rituals provided structure before every point and helped me deal with my nervousness. Rituals also gave me a framework in which to play the same way I had practiced.

Billie Jean King told me that tennis rituals are paramount to a player's game because they give discipline and comfort. The thing you don't want, Billie Jean said, is to become *over*dependent on rituals to the point that if you don't straighten out your strings or check your shock absorber between points, you can't play.

When we talk about having "rituals" in our spiritual lives, just the mention of the word can raise eyebrows. In the past, religious rituals placed emphasis on ceremony and rites: that if we worship God in a prescribed order, then He will look with favor upon us. True Christianity doesn't work that way. We can't "work" our way to heaven. Instead, my idea of a good ritual is starting off the day with some quiet time with God, reading His Word and lifting up our needs to Him. I've had friends tell me that they read one Psalm and one chapter of Proverbs (there are thirty-one) each morning with their cereal and coffee.

Now that sounds like a ritual worth practicing to me . . .

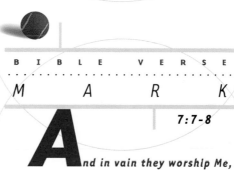

B I B L E   V E R S E
. . . .

M   A   R   K

7:7-8

And in vain they worship Me, teaching as doctrines the commandments of men. For laying aside the commandment of God, you hold the tradition of men — the washing of pitchers and cups, and many other such things you do.

WHEN GOD DOESN'T MAKE SENSE

I first met my close friend Monica Seles when she was a twelve-year-old phenom whacking groundstrokes down the street from my Orlando home. Her coach at the time, Nick Bollettieri, stacked pyramids of tennis balls in the back corners of the court and told Monica to swing away. She nailed the targets with uncanny precision.

When Monica began playing professional tennis tournaments a few years later, I befriended her when few players on the tour would acknowledge her. The other players saw Monica as a threat, perhaps because she *was* a threat. While she was still Sweet Sixteen, Monica cranked her two-handed forehands and backhands into high gear to capture her first Grand Slam — the French Open. At seventeen, she became the youngest

No. 1 player of all time.

The way Monica was collecting Grand Slam silverware — she held up various U.S. Open, French Open, and Australian Open winner's trophies and plates eight times in the early 1990s — many felt she would one day be called the greatest female tennis player ever. As for our friendship, something just clicked. I liked making her laugh, doing fun things like teaching her how to drive a car with a stick shift, or just hanging out with her away from the tennis court.

Then, in 1993 came a stunning news flash from Hamburg, Germany — someone had attacked Monica during a changeover, stabbing her in the back. For the next twenty-four hours, newscasts played the horrific tape of the assault: the balding man reaching from the stands with a gleaming knife in his right hand; Monica reacting in disbelief as she reached over her shoulder to touch her back; the waves of pain riveting through her body as she straightened up and tried to walk; the shocked Monica falling to her knees while Lisa Gratton, a tour official, held her close and called for help.

Monica, falling in and out of consciousness and her tennis shirt dripping with blood, was rushed to a nearby hospital for treatment. Meanwhile, Günther Parche, a German fan of Steffi Graf, was whisked into custody. News reports quoted him as saying that he stabbed Monica because he wanted to help Steffi reclaim her No. 1 position.

Bizarre! The stabbing sent shivers down my spine and shock waves around the world. I can remember falling on my bed, praying for Monica's safety, asking the Lord why such a nice person like Monica — the planet's best tennis player at the height of her power — deserved to be stabbed. Why would God allow a deranged man to lean out of the stands and thrust a nine-inch knife into Monica's upper back? Why would an innocent young woman come within a few millimeters of losing her life or being paralyzed forever?

Monica soon recovered from the physical wounds, but the mental wounds haunted her. She retreated behind the walls of her walled-off Florida estate. I reached out to her, but darkness enveloped her life as she quietly sought life's shadows. For more than a year, she rarely ventured out in public, preferring to leave the drapes closed and her life hidden from the public.

I kept encouraging Monica during that dark time, not because I wanted her to return to the game she loved, but because I loved her like a sister. I continued to pray for her and be a good friend.

After Monica hit a few balls in bare feet on my backyard court, my husband Mark and I invited her and her father, Karolj, to come over and play some hit-and-giggle mixed doubles with us. I can't remember who won that afternoon, but I do remember the laughter and enjoyment. I don't know who was happier — Monica or Karolj. Monica eventually made a triumphant return to women's tennis, but she didn't win as often as before. Günther Parche got his wish. The tragedy is that we will never know how many more Grand Slam championships Monica would have won if she hadn't been stabbed.

Why did God allow Monica to be pierced with a knife? Why does God allow natural disasters, famines, disease, and world wars? I've struggled with that because we do not know the answers — only the all-knowing Lord of the Universe knows why. We do know that these things are not God's perfect will, but in this life we may never know the "whys." That is the exact place where faith begins

— believing without seeing.

What I also know is that disastrous or horrific situations are great times to have the Lord as part of your life. Only God can take a giant eraser and wipe away the pain or anger or unforgiveness or fear. There is no humanly possible way that we can erase these things, but God can — and He promises us that He will.

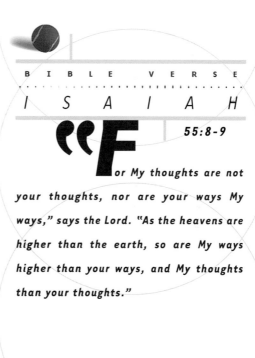

B I B L E   V E R S E

I   S   A   I   A   H

55:8-9

For My thoughts are not your thoughts, nor are your ways My ways," says the Lord. "As the heavens are higher than the earth, so are My ways higher than your ways, and My thoughts than your thoughts."

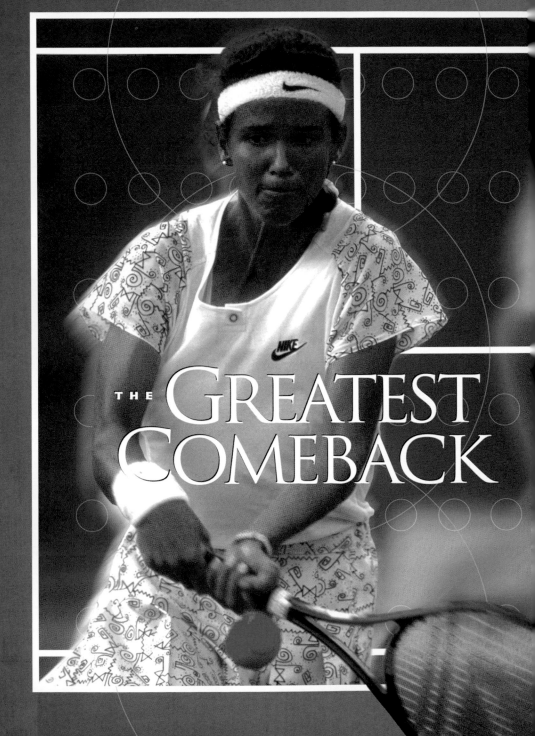

THE GREATEST COMEBACK

"Thirty seconds, and then we come to you," I heard the ESPN producer say. I pressed my headset closer to my ears and waited for us to come out of a commercial.

I was sitting in a broadcast booth above Court 1 at Roland Garros, site of the French Open tennis tournament. Barry Tompkins, my broadcast partner at ESPN, straightened up in his seat as we prepared to go live to the United States.

"Welcome, everybody, to this quarterfinal match between Mary Joe Fernandez of the United States and Gabriella Sabatini of Argentina," began Barry. "These two players have been playing each other a long time, haven't they, Betsy?"

"That's right, Barry. They first ran into each other at the Orange Bowl junior tournament when they were twelve years old," I replied. "They're good friends; they speak Spanish to each other, but this is probably the biggest match of their long rivalry. The winner advances to the semifinals where Arantxa Sanchez-Vicario is waiting . . ."

Gabriella began the match as though she were double-parked and in a hurry. She quickly raced to a 3-love lead, so ESPN switched to Court Central, where Pete Sampras was locked in a marquee struggle with Sergi Bruguera, a young Spanish player. Cliff Drysdale and the "Fiery One," Fred Stolle, had the call for that men's fourth-round match on ESPN.

Meanwhile, Barry and I continued to monitor Mary Joe's match with Gaby, as friends called Sabatini. Mary Joe was getting shellacked. After twenty minutes, ESPN coverage came back our way.

"We're at 5-1, set point for Gabriella Sabatini," said Barry on the air.

"You don't see Mary Joe get outclassed like this very often, but she hasn't been able to do anything right today," I noted.

Coverage returned to Court Central, and I knew that unless Mary Joe turned things around quickly, we wouldn't be on the air very long. Twenty-five minutes later, I heard the umpire intone, *Jeu, Mademoiselle Sabatini. Elle mène cinq jeu á un, deuxième manche.* I didn't need a French translation. Mary Joe was down 6-1, 5-1, just a few points from elimination.

Since Gaby was about to close out the match, ESPN coverage bounced over to us. All she had to do was serve it out, and she could head for the locker room. Meanwhile, Mary Joe smoothed the red *terre batue* surface with her shoe, trying to find her focus. She hadn't been playing poorly in my estimation, but her shots were just missing the

lines. She looked at the on-court clock. They had played fifty-five minutes. Mary Joe told me later that she had made it a goal to stretch the match out to at least an hour. That became her motivation in an embarrassing situation.

At 40-30, Gaby had reached match point.

Then came a doublefault.

"A reprieve, but probably not for long," I commented.

Then Mary Joe broke serve and held to bring the set score to 5-3. Her strokes had more sting and greater accuracy.

"Gabriella has to be careful here because she's only ahead by one break," I noted. Evidently, Gabriella wasn't careful enough because she dropped serve, thanks to some inspired play by Mary Joe.

ESPN couldn't leave us now. We had a comeback going. As the capacity crowd of six thousand exhorted her, Mary Joe took the second set in a tiebreaker.

"We've got ourselves a match!" I exclaimed into the commercial break. Mary Joe, who's a wonderful young Christian woman, did some-thing from which we can all learn. When she was down in the pits, way behind at 6-1, 5-1, she set a short-term goal: *Keep her out here for at least one hour.* Instead of looking at the seemingly insurmountable task of winning that match, her immediate goal was to prolong the second set as long as she could.

Mary Joe had some work ahead of her if she wanted to make an unlikely comeback. Neither player could gain a lead in the final set. They played to 7-7 and 8-8. (There's no tiebreaker in the deciding set at the French Open.) Then Mary Joe squandered a handful of match points.

"She's waiting for Gaby to make the error," I commented. "She will have to go for it if she gets a chance."

On Mary Joe's fifth match point, she smacked a service return that skidded off the sideline.

"She's done it!" said Barry Tompkins. The cameras zoomed in on two bone-tired competitors embracing each other instead of shaking hands while the umpire announced the score in Mary Joe's favor: 1-6, 7-5, 10-8. Match time: three-and-a-half hours of grueling tennis.

Mary Joe decided to break down an overwhelming lead into something more manageable, which gave her a victory. Short-term goals are just as applicable to our spiritual lives.

Spiritually, we can become overwhelmed when we think our problems are so huge, so gigantic, that there's no way we'll ever conquer these difficulties and become victorious. Yet if we break things down and try to get through the next minute or the next hour or the next day, God can work in our situation. No lead is too great for the Lord Almighty. If we find ourselves in an impossible situation, we can call on Jesus, who tells us that we can do all things through Him who strengthens us (Phil. 4:13).

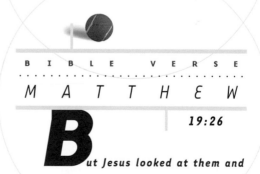

BIBLE VERSE

MATTHEW

19:26

But Jesus looked at them and said to them, "With men this is impossible, but with God all things are possible."

DAVID vs. GOLIATH in PARIS

CHAPTER 13

We don't know how old David was when the chair umpire introduced him and his opponent — a hard-hitting giant named Goliath — but this wet-behind-the-ears Hebrew still had to be in the junior ranks. Yet David had told his coach, Saul, "Don't worry about a thing. I will take care of this Philistine!"

"Don't be ridiculous!" Saul replied. "There is no way you can go against this Philistine. You are only a boy, and he has been in the army since he was a boy!"

We all know the outcome — David killed his adversary with a huge serve that astonished thousands of spectators, including those sitting in the Royal Box. The ATP Tour radar gun clocked the rock at 152 mph, a new record, and Goliath never knew what hit him. Game, set, and match, David, in a walkover.

The David-vs.-Goliath metaphor was never more apt than when young Michael Chang took the court against the world's No. 1 player, a dour-faced Ivan Lendl, in a round-of-sixteen match at the French Open in 1989. Here was a seventeen-year-old boy sent to do battle with a bigger, more experienced, implacable Czech who *enjoyed* grinding opponents into the ground. At 5'8" and 135 pounds, Michael appeared to be a mere child against his older, more physically imposing foe. It didn't matter that Michael had been the youngest player to win the U.S. Juniors at fifteen years old, the same year he became the youngest player to win a match at the U.S. Open. Nor was Lendl intimated by the fact that Michael was the youngest in sixty years to play on Centre Court at Wimbledon (at sixteen) or the youngest in sixty-one years to play on a U.S. Davis Cup team (also at sixteen). Lendl would get on top of Michael and pound him into submission.

And that's exactly what happened for the first two sets, which Lendl won. When most players lose the first two sets of a best-of-five-set match, they begin to wonder if they can catch the late-afternoon flight back home. Not Michael. He fought and scraped to work himself back into the match, counterpunching each Lendl fusillade and retrieving the Czech's toughest shots.

A murmur swept through Roland Garros when Michael fought back

to win sets three and four. Yet it was Michael who was in trouble at the start of the fifth set. Michael began cramping so badly that he could barely move. When your legs cramp — either from exhaustion or nervous tension — you feel as though someone has inserted steel rods in them. Somehow Michael persevered and kept the ball in play. A bewildered Lendl refused to hit for the corners, try a delicate drop shot, or otherwise take the net against his cramping adversary.

The fifth set remained close while Michael chomped on bananas and gulped water during changeover. He couldn't sit down, lest he risk not being able to stand up again. Somehow, Michael managed to take a 4-3 lead with a service break in hand. Lendl worked himself to a 15-30 lead against Michael's serve. Ivan was thinking, *A couple of more points, it will be 4-4, with me serving . . .*

Michael stepped up to serve at 15-30, which players call the "swing point." Win it, and it's 30-30, and the advantage returns to the server. Lose it, and you're down two huge break points.

Michael suddenly quick-wristed an *underhand* serve with side spin. The ball took a strange bounce, and all Lendl could do was chip a weak backhand down the line, which he halfheartedly followed to the net. Michael dipped a topspin forehand down the line. Lendl awkwardly reached for the passing shot and watched the ball glance off his racket.

The crowd roared at this playground ploy! As for Lendl, he was as destroyed mentally by the missed shot as Goliath was physically by the stone. He screamed invectives at the chair umpire and to the heavens. While Lendl continued to complain, he lost the game and quickly fell behind 15-40 on his serve. Match point.

Lendl faulted on his first serve. The sellout crowd was hushed to silence by the umpire. Wait a minute! What's Michael doing? He's hobbling to within a couple of feet of the service box. He's going to return serve right next to the service line!

Lendl, surprised as much as anyone by Michael's boldness, paused and tried to regain his composure. After four hours and thirty-seven minutes of battle, Lendl cracked when he ricocheted the serve off the net cord and out of the service box. Michael fell to his knees sobbing, and he left the court in tears. He later collapsed in the training room.

The rest of the story is history — great tennis history. Michael went on to win the French Open that year and become the youngest male to win a Grand Slam singles title at the age of seventeen. He readily credited his victory to "the Lord Jesus Christ," although most reporters dropped their gaze and stopped writing when he gave Christ the glory.

One of the first things that Michael did upon his return home was attend a thanksgiving service at the Chinese Christian Church in Thousand Oaks, California, where his grandfather was a founding member. The congregation cheered wildly when Michael was asked to say a few words. Michael explained that all those come-from-behind victories in Paris weren't coincidences.

"That wasn't me playing out there," Michael shared. "Jesus Christ is alive and well."

1 SAMUEL

17:45-47

Then David said to the Philistine, "You come to me with a sword, with a spear, and with a javelin. But I come to you in the name of the Lord of hosts, the God of the armies of Israel, whom you have defied. This day the Lord will deliver you into my hand, and I will strike you and take your head from you. And this day I will give the carcasses of the camp of the Philistines to the birds of the air and the wild beasts of the earth, that all the earth may know that there is a God in Israel. Then all this assembly shall know that the Lord does not save with sword and spear; for the battle is the Lord's, and He will give you into our hands."

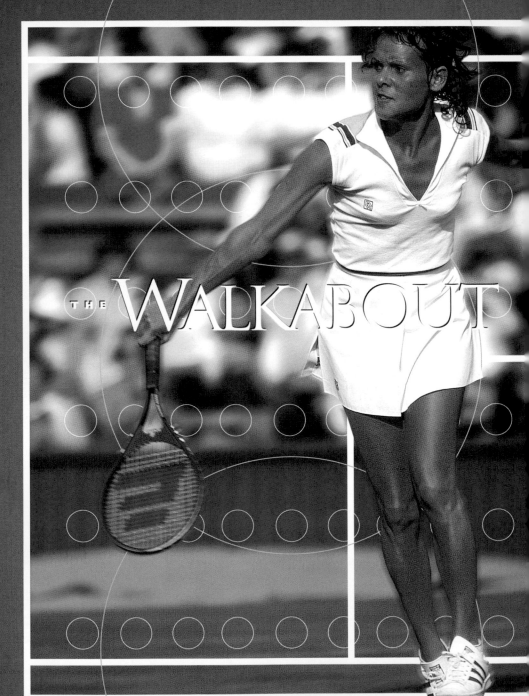

CHAPTER 14

Before Aboriginal runner Cathy Freeman captured the hearts of 3.7 billion people who watched her light the Olympic flame at the 2000 Summer Games in Sydney, Australia, and later win a gold medal in the 400 meters, tennis gave the sporting world its first Aboriginal champion — Evonne Goolagong.

Evonne, a contemporary of mine, was born in 1951 in a country town called Barellan in New South Wales. Her father, Ken, sheared sheep while her mum, Linda, tended after a herd of kids — Evonne and her seven brothers and sisters. The Goolagongs were the only "dark people," as neighbors called them, in Barellan.

Evonne was a Wiradjuri Aborigine, a descendent of a culture that populated Australia long before a shipload of English

prisoners dumped in Sydney Harbor in 1788 became the first British settlement. This event marked the start of more than two hundred years of official mistreatment and second-class citizenship.

Evonne was unaware of this history when she started hitting a tennis ball against a house wall when she was five years old. Actually, their house was an abandoned tin shack with worn-out, ink-blotched linoleum floors. A tomboy, Evonne began beating the boys at all sorts of games. She started playing tennis, and because she was such a talent, the local people let her join the tennis club.

By the age of ten, Evonne decided that she wanted to become a Wimbledon champion. She began traveling to Sydney for coaching by Vic Edwards, a legend in Australian tennis circles. He invited her to live in his family's home for further coaching. During her teen years, Evonne won thirty-seven Australian junior tournaments, including many doubles titles with her coach's daughter, Trisha Edwards.

Evonne trained very hard. At eighteen, Vic decided she was ready for Wimbledon, but Evonne lost in the second round. Although this was a good result for a young player, Evonne continued to have up-and-down matches during her rookie season. In fact, it was the *way* she lost her matches that drove her coach crazy.

Evonne's success seemed to depend on the skill of her opponent. Her interest level stayed up when strong players challenged her, but if her adversary wasn't that good, a fog seemed to come over her. Her concentration vanished in a haze of inattention. She lost games quickly. Whenever Evonne began losing her grip on a match, her chain-smoking coach, Vic, could be heard muttering something about "Evonne's gone walkabout."

Tennis journalists picked up Edwards' "walkabout" phrase, and *walkabout* became shorthand for a fade-out, a retreat, a mental withdrawal, or blown concentration. So when nineteen-year-old Evonne Goolagong surprised the tennis world by advancing to the Ladies Singles final at Wimbledon in 1971, the press speculated before the match whether Evonne would experience another walkabout or would hang tough against compatriot Margaret Court, a three-time Wimbledon winner.

Evonne hung tough. She rode an early break to a 6-4 first set victory, at which point everyone waited for her to start waltzing Matilda, but she never did. Evonne sailed through the second 6-1 to win her first of two Wimbledon crowns and five Grand Slam titles. Later, when Evonne Goolagong Cawley beat Chris Evert in 1980 to win Wimbledon, she was the mom of a toddler. We may never see a mom win Wimbledon again!

The term "walkabout" can be applied to our spiritual lives as well. Do you go through life in a fog, choosing to put God in a box while you fight life's battles alone? Do you have trouble concentrating when you're involved in prayer or studying God's Word? The Christian life involves a recognition that God desires fellowship with us continually, not just a few minutes between songs on Sunday mornings. It's also not going "walkabout" the rest of the week. The Christian walk means spending time in prayer and reading the Bible daily. "Your word is a lamp to my feet and a light for my path," Psalm 119 says. Proverbs 4:12 says, "When you walk, your steps will not be hindered, and when you run, you will not stumble." That doesn't sound like a walkabout to me.

If someone were to ask how your walk with Christ was going, what would *you* say?

PSALMS

23:4-6

Yea, though I walk through the valley of the shadow of death, I will fear no evil; for You are with me; Your rod and Your staff, they comfort me. You prepare a table before me in the presence of my enemies; You anoint my head with oil; my cup runs over. Surely goodness and mercy shall follow me all the days of my life; and I will dwell in the house of the Lord forever.

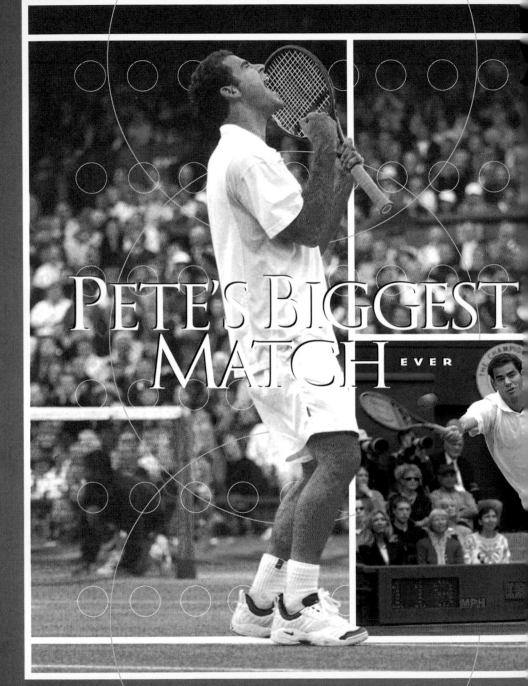

PETE'S BIGGEST MATCH EVER

15

I don't know whether tennis historians will judge Pete Sampras to be tennis' greatest male player after he uncoils his final serve, but the player who breaks his record of thirteen Grand Slam singles titles probably hasn't been born yet. Pete eclipsed the record of Roy Emerson, but Emmo's dozen "majors" were won in the 1960s before the game opened up to professionals.

Pete broke the record in the summer of 2000 in front of 13,812 spectators packed into Wimbledon's Centre Court. At 9 p.m. local time with darkness settling in, Pete bombed in another unreturnable serve against Australia's Patrick Rafter. Pete raised his arms in triumph, shook hands with Rafter, walked over to his chair, and put down his racket. Then he stepped back on the tennis court to take a

bow. The normally impassive Pete let the tears flow as waves of applause washed over him.

Then Pete searched Centre Court grandstand for his parents, Sam and Georgia, who were fighting back their own tears. The Wimbledon champ left the greensward and climbed thick, wide steps to bear hug his father and mother. They had not been sitting in the "Friend's Box" but were in the main grandstand underneath the overhang.

Sam and Georgia had literally arrived at the last minute to watch their son play for history, having taken an overnight flight from Los Angeles that touched down in London that morning. You could say that Sam and Georgia are the opposite of the "pushy" tennis parents that seem to populate the tour. In fact, the Samprases have seen their progeny play in person only a couple of times during his long, storied career.

Sam, especially, professes to be too nervous to watch. When Pete played for his first Grand Slam title in the 1990 U.S. Open at the age of nineteen, he and Georgia strolled a Los Angeles mall during the match because they couldn't bear to watch on TV. I shudder to think what could have happened to Sam if he and Georgia had passed a bank of TVs at Sears that Sunday afternoon!

Pete's 2000 Wimbledon match was the first one that his parents had witnessed in eight years. What makes this even more interesting is that the last time Sam and Georgia saw Pete play happened at the 1992 U.S. Open — a match that Pete later said was the most important of his career.

The U.S. Open is the only major that requires its men's semifinal winners to play the final on the following day. Normally, you have a rest day between the semis and finals, but on "Super Saturday," the U.S. Open sandwiches the two men's semifinals around the women's final. (In recent years, the women's final has been the final match of the day.)

In 1992, Pete drew the late match against Jim Courier. They battled deep into the night, and by the fifth set, Pete's body was running on empty. Suffering from severe stomach cramps in the closing two games, Pete barely got past Courier. Pete was rushed to the trainer's room, where he was given an IV and treated for dehydration while he battled diarrhea. By the time Pete reached his hotel and nodded off to sleep, it was 3:30 a.m.

When Pete woke up five hours later, the upset stomach was still there. Waiting for him was a stiff Stefan Edberg (who had played a marathon five-hour, twenty-two-minute match against Michael Chang the previous day). Sam and Georgia looked on as Pete tried to gut out his match against Edberg, but a weakening body and rash of double-faults doomed him to a tough four-set loss.

The storyline taken by many in the media that day was that Pete, with just one Grand Slam victory two years earlier, was a "one-hit wonder," a player of great promise who might never win a Big One again. Pete's terrible disappointment in that loss, however, resulted in a major turning point in his career.

"Before that match, I didn't hate to lose," said Pete, adding that the bitter taste of losing to Edberg provided him with the motivation he needed to train more seriously and take his game to the next level. No longer would he say, "I ran out of gas," as he did that afternoon at Flushing Meadow. He would discipline himself on the practice court — and go on to make tennis history.

Scripture tells us that, "Now no chastening seems to be joyful for the present, but painful; nevertheless, afterward it yields the peaceable fruit of righteousness to those who have been trained by it." (Heb. 12:11). Many of us — and I place myself squarely in this camp — have to go through life learning things the hard way. It's what we do after we experience disappointment and defeat that determines whether we grow stronger as a result of them.

Disappointments or defeats lurking in our backgrounds can — and *should* — prompt us to become more self-disciplined. I know that my spiritual fitness improves when I'm reading my Bible each day, having a regular quiet time listening to the Lord, holding to my Monday Bible study held at my home, and attending biblically based conferences. If you're experiencing difficulties in staying spiritually disciplined, start with ten minutes of reading God's Word each day and listening to what He wants to say to you.

Do so, and you'll start producing a harvest of righteousness faster than a Pete Sampras service ace!

BIBLE VERSE

PROVERBS
15:32

He who disdains instruction despises his own soul, but he who heeds rebuke gets understanding.

TREASURES IN HEAVEN

CHAPTER

16

"And now," as radio broadcaster Paul Harvey would say, "here is 'The Rest of the Story.'"

San Benito, Texas, is a farming town in the lower tip of the Lone Star State where in the mid-1950s, citrus and vegetables were the cash crops. It was a time of flat tops, bobby sox, and hot rods. Jim, a high school senior, was the No. 1 tennis player on the high school team.

In south Texas, you could play tennis year-round, if you didn't mind the broiling heat of summertime or the chilly winds that whipped through the lower Rio Grande River valley in the winter months. As long as it wasn't blazing hot or too cold, Jim played six days a week, two or three hours a day, and all day Saturday. Dressed in white shorts, a white T-shirt, and Jack Purcell sneakers, Jim honed his game to become the best player in his small town.

When Jim graduated from high school, he wanted to attend a college sponsored by his church denomination. Pasadena College, a small Christian liberal arts institution of higher learning out in California, looked promising, even though it was two thousand miles from home.

Jim applied and was accepted, and the big day arrived for him to pack his trunk and belongings — including his trusty wood racket — for the long drive out west. He followed Route 66 through New Mexico and Arizona before arriving in Pasadena, a sleepy Los Angeles suburb that was home to the Rose Parade every January 1.

He arrived on campus before the other students and decided to get the lay of the land. With his hands in his pockets on this September day in 1954, Jim came upon the Administration Building, where he viewed a large trophy case just inside the entryway.

Jim stepped up to the glass case filled with trophies and plaques from past years of sporting glory. Many commemorated the championship basketball teams that had represented Pasadena College. Then his eyes focused on a large trophy standing resolutely in the center of the glass case. It commanded his attention.

Standing two feet tall with a replica of a tennis player affixed to the top, the spiral trophy was inscribed with the names of the Pasadena College school champions of yesteryear. Immortalized for posterity, this roll call of Pasadena College tennis champions read like Tilden, Riggs, and Kramer to the young freshman from Texas.

Jim scanned the names, almost as if he were committing them to memory. "Someday," he vowed to himself, "my name will be engraved on this trophy as the best tennis player in this school. Ten, twenty, thirty

years from now, people will look at this trophy and see *my* name listed among the tennis greats of Pasadena College."

Jim didn't win the school tournament in his freshman or sophomore years. All his practice and hard work paid off, though, when he won the annual Pasadena College competition in his junior year. Jim thought he would never be so proud as the day when the perpetual trophy was inscribed with his name next to "1957." For good measure and to confirm his athletic prowess, Jim defeated all comers at the 1958 Pasadena College school championships. He had successfully defended his title, ensuring his legacy for future generations.

Twenty-five years pass. A young Pasadena College student, rummaging through the trash, finds a dented trophy with the replica of a tennis player on the top. He recognizes the name of the 1957 winner of the Pasadena College Tennis Championship — a person who was now a best-selling author, host of a radio program heard daily by more than a million people, and founder of a ministry that touches millions of families around the globe. The young student salvages the trophy so that he can return it to the former Pasadena champion.

Standing in his office, Dr. James Dobson, the president and founder of Focus on the Family, holds the redeemed trophy — now scratched and dented — in the palms of his hands. *The school didn't even record my 1958 victory*, he thinks.

But Dr. Dobson hears an inner voice that says, *If you live long enough, life will trash your trophies.* It's another reminder that only two things matter: serving God and being acceptable to Him on that Day of Judgment.

I would have liked to have been in Dr. Dobson's office when he received that old tennis tournament trophy. I'm sure we could have shared a good laugh because I was just like young James Dobson at one time — determined to make my mark in the tennis world and be immortalized for generations. But do the names Betty Nuthall, Molla Bjurstedt, or Evelyn Sears mean anything to you? They won Wimbledon during the twentieth century. How about Charlotte Sterry, Blanche Hillyard, or Muriel Robb? They are past U.S. Open winners.

I wonder what these great players of the past think is important now that they are gone? It certainly isn't answering the roll call of Grand Slam champions. I am reminded of the psalmist who wrote, "As for man, his days are like grass, he flourishes like a flower of the field; the wind blows over it and it is gone, and its place remembers it no more" (Ps. 103: 15-16).

And now you know "The Rest of the Story."

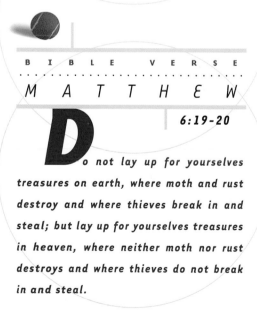

BIBLE VERSE

MATTHEW

6:19-20

Do not lay up for yourselves treasures on earth, where moth and rust destroy and where thieves break in and steal; but lay up for yourselves treasures in heaven, where neither moth nor rust destroys and where thieves do not break in and steal.

TENSION
IN ROMANIA

The fall of 1972 was an anxious time to be a world-class athlete — especially if you were Jewish — because of what happened in the early morning hours of September 5, 1972. Eight Arab commandos broke into the Olympic Village in the midst of the Olympic Games in Munich, West Germany, shooting and killing two Israelis and holding nine members of the Israeli Olympic team hostage.

When negotiations failed to gain the hostages' release, the terrorists agreed to leave the Olympic compound for the Fursten-feldbruck military airport, where they planned to fly with their captives to an Arab-friendly country. Then gunfire broke out between the West German sharpshooters and the comman-dos, who immediately began shooting their hostages. When the firestorm was over, all nine Israeli hostages had been executed, and five Arab commandos had been killed, while three suffered gunshot wounds.

Five weeks later the U.S. Davis Cup team, with two Jewish members, Harold Solomon and Brian Gottfried, touched down in Bucharest, Romania, for the long-awaited, final-round Davis Cup match between the two countries. This would be the biggest sporting event ever played on Romanian soil. With the eyes of the world focused on Bucharest, President Nicolae Ceausescu, a hard-line Communist, would brook no "incidents." He ordered his secret police to escort the U.S. contingent everywhere. Security was tighter than a gut-string job.

U.S. team Captain Dennis Ralston says the team never stopped for a red light during their entire stay, and the secret police even followed the players into the restrooms.

"At first, it was funny," Dennis recalled, "but on the last day of the Davis Cup tie, the police found two people trying to scale the walls of the tennis stadium. When I asked what happened, I was told that the authorities had 'disappeared' them."

Romania had never won a Davis Cup in the history of the nation-against-nation competition. Here was a golden chance, with tough players Ilie Nastase and Ion Tiriac on their side. Nastase was ranked No. 2 in the world. As for Tiriac, a book could be written about this colorful character with a mean streak. The players nicknamed "Nasty" and "Count Dracula" would bring the Cup home.

Ceausescu ordered the Army to build a special stadium for the three-day match, and the linesmen chairs were filled with patriotic Romanians who felt obliged to make the "right call" for the home team. Perhaps that's why the night before the first match, the "neutral" referee,

Enrique Morea of Argentina, told Stan Smith, "You have to win easily."

"What do you mean, win easily?" Stan replied.

"Because I'm not going to change any calls," Enrique said.

"If you're not going to change any calls, then who is?" Stan queried.

With that, Enrique shrugged his shoulders.

Knowing what he had to do, Stan played splendid tennis in the opening rubber against Nastase, shattering the Romanian's fragile psyche by winning handily in what was expected to be a very difficult match. Next up was Tom Gorman versus Ion Tiriac — a must-win match for the Romanians. As the match progressed, the line calls became more and more ridiculous. It was obvious to Captain Ralston that his players were getting cheated. After all, the ball leaves a large imprint every time it strikes the red clay, and Dennis could only hold his face in his hands as the calls piled up against Tom. Compounding his misery were the rabid Romanian fans, who yelled and stomped their feet between each point.

The American captain stewed while Tom suffered indignity after indignity. *His player was getting hooked out of the match!* Anytime Tom hit the ball near the line, a Romanian line judge yelled "Out!" Conversely, the court was six inches longer and wider for Tiriac. Since players are trained from a young age to "hit for the lines," Tom was reduced to fighting a lion of a player without a chair and a whip.

Late in the fourth set, Tom lost his serve on the umpteenth horrendous call, and Dennis was losing his mind. Davis Cup captains sit on the court and coach players during changeovers — and stick up for their players during disputed line calls.

On this particular changeover, Tiriac passed by the captain with a smirk that said, *I know you're getting cheated, but there's nothing you can do about it. I am going to win this match.* Dennis reached for one of Tom's spare Head rackets. He decided that if Ion made any sort of move on him, he would whack him with a racket.

"I was that far gone," said Dennis. "I was an instant away from decking Tiriac with Gorman's racket, and that would have been the end of our team. We would have created an international incident, and the U.S. team would have been defaulted."

Tiriac kept moving and didn't make eye contact. The moment passed. Dennis sat back in his on-court chair and put the racket aside.

Tom Gorman ended up losing the match, and to this day, Dennis wonders what prompted Ion Tiriac not to make a move on him. The Davis Cup captain believes it was the Lord's protection. At the time, Dennis was struggling to make sense of his life. His wife, Linda, had become a Christian; Dennis could not discount the changes he saw in her life. While in Romania, Dennis began a spiritual journey that started with reading the Bible. The verse that resonated with him was Romans 8:28, which, incidentally, was the Scripture that changed my life and caused me to become a Christian.

The Americans may have lost that match, but the Davis Cup tie wasn't over. Even more importantly, Dennis Ralston found eternal life.

B I B L E   V E R S E
. . . .

R O M A N S

8:28

And we know that in all things God works for the good of those who love Him, who have been called according to His purpose.

ROMANIA: THE ANXIETY CONTINUES

After the United States and Romania split the opening singles matches in the 1972 Davis Cup finals, Ion Tiriac gave the Americans a "one-in-ten" chance of defeating Romania on its home court. Everyone expected Ion Tiriac and Ilie Nastase to steamroll Stan Smith and partner Erik Van Dillen in the doubles, but the Americans played the match of their lives under tremendous pressure, defeating the Romanians in three straight sets.

The United States needed to win only one more rubber to bring home the Davis Cup, but since Ilie Nastase would never lose to a lower-ranked player like Tom Gorman in their match, both sides knew the winner of the Stan Smith-Ion Tiriac match would decide the tie. Stan, a Christian since his teenage days, knew that Tiriac would bring every gamesmanship weapon to the court. A bushy-headed Transylvanian known as "Count Dracula," Tiriac played hockey as a youth and was good enough to win a spot on the Romanian Olympic hockey team in 1964. A late bloomer on the tennis court, his bullheaded tenacity and on-court gamesmanship allowed him to become — in self-described terms — the "greatest player who couldn't play."

Armed with a weird scoop-shovel forehand and chip backhand, Ion drove opponents crazy. One demoralized opponent, down match point to the Romanian, blooped a sitter to Ion, who was standing at the net. Instead of swatting the floater away and ending the match, he caught the ball.

"It is so pitiful. I can't take this point," Ion said. Talk about psychological mind games! Most imposing was Tiriac's dark, swarthy moustache that wrapped around his jowls like a black centipede. A flat forehead, coupled with a perpetual glare, turned him into a larger-than-life figure.

Heading onto the court in Budapest, Stan knew he would need every ounce of concentration that he possessed. The head games started even before the match, when Romanian tennis officials presented Tiriac with a three-foot trophy commemorating his 100th Davis Cup match.

Tiriac came out hot, taking the first set, but more importantly, controlling the situation. He constantly interrupted the flow of the match by conversing with Argentinian referee Enrique Morea and with the Romanian linesmen. Stan felt like Tiriac was orchestrating some monkey business, but he couldn't be sure.

Stan soon became aware that any of his shots close to the line wouldn't be called his way. He had heard that he should stand and serve a good six inches or even a foot behind the baseline, lest he be called for a footfault. In an earlier match between Romania and Australia, a Romanian linesman had called numerous second-serve footfaults on break point, which, of course, resulted in the automatic loss of the game. Stan decided to serve hard and hope for the best.

Stan regained control in the second set and won. He continued to outplay Ion in the pivotal third set, building a 5-3 lead. Tiriac broke back, however, and was serving at 4-5, 40-love as the Romanian crowd whipped themselves into a frenzy. "Teer-ee-ack,! Teer-ee-ack!" they screamed, while the umpire just looked at his scorecard. Stan felt like the match was slipping out of his grasp.

Suddenly, Tiriac lost a couple of points. Stan worked his way back to deuce, then earned a set point. Advantage United States. Tiriac hit a first serve that was a little long. Stan, who was playing everything, knocked a backhand up the line for a clean winner. Tiriac stormed the net and demanded that the linesman call the serve out, and the linesman complied. It had to be the latest "out" call in history.

On the second serve, Tiriac dumped the ball halfway up the net. There was no way a linesman could change that result. Third set to the United States.

The fourth set was all Tiriac. At one point, the Romanian hit a drop shot. Stan ran for his life, but he didn't reach the ball before it bounced twice. In frustration, he slammed the ball into the net. Tiriac then began arguing with the referee that Stan was trying to hit him, which riled up the crowd to a fever pitch. Tiriac began stalling. When the umpire motioned for him to play, Tiriac said, "Go ahead and default me. Then see what happens!" Referee Enrique begged him to return to the court.

The stage was set for a climactic fifth set. Stan served the first game, but quickly dug himself into a big hole — down 15-40. Both sides knew that if Tiriac got a break, he and the Romanian crowd would not be denied. Stan looked over to U.S. Team Captain Dennis Ralston. *Stay calm, stay calm,* Dennis motioned with his palms downward.

To this day, Stan can't remember what happened next. But the record shows that Stan served himself out of the jam, and he rode the momentum to a 6-0 final set triumph. As he walked to the net after the final point, he wondered if he should shake hands with his bitter opponent. Stan decided to, but he had a message for his foe.

"I don't respect you as a person anymore," Stan said, turning his back and walking away.

Dennis Ralston believes that epic match — with its symbolization of Communist control vs. freedom — was a battle of good triumphing over evil. Stan doesn't quite see it in those terms. He was busy playing the match, not watching it.

"Honestly, I know that Stan is the only guy who could have won that match," Dennis said. "I don't even think Rod Laver could have remained as calm or stayed as focused as Stan did that afternoon. What kept Stan going was his deep reservoir of faith."

With God on his side, even under the gazes of thousands of rabid Romanians, Stan Smith prevailed.

BIBLE VERSE

MARK

9:23

Jesus said to him, "If you can believe, all things are possible to him who believes."

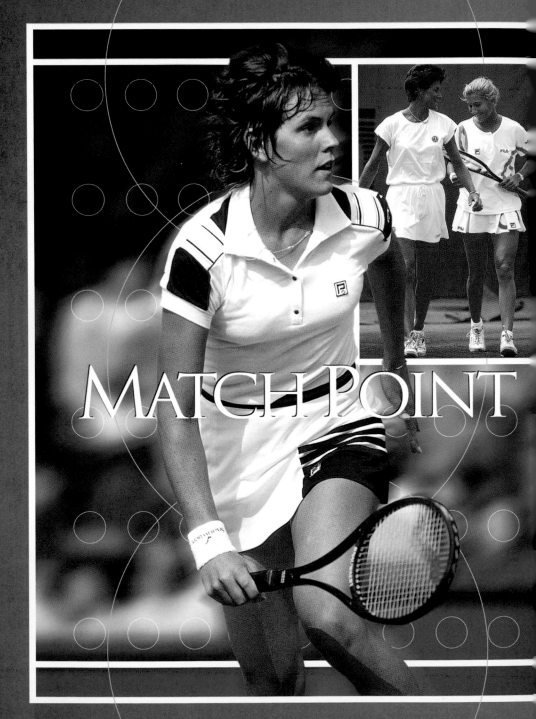

MATCH POINT

CHAPTER

"There is a time for everything, and a season for every activity under heaven," wrote Solomon in Ecclesiastes.

I surely understand that passage of Scripture better today than when I spent much of my life running around the world, chasing a fuzzy optic yellow ball and little else.

I was born Betsy Nagelsen in the fall of 1956 and grew up in tennis-rich St. Petersburg, Florida, with a Wilson Pro Staff wood racket in my right hand. My mom, Marty, couldn't keep me off the public courts at Bartlett Park Tennis Center. By the time I was eight years old, I had taken an avid interest in the game. I began playing junior tournaments throughout Florida and scored some success.

Keep in mind that the late 1960s and early '70s were much simpler times. Tennis had just gone "open" (in other words, professionals were allowed to enter any tournament), and the sport was gaining fans and players right and left. When a fellow Floridian, Chris Evert, made a big splash at the 1971 U.S. Open at the age of sixteen, I wanted to be the next teen sensation to come out of the Sunshine State.

Winning the U.S. National 18s — the biggest title in junior tennis — was the springboard I needed to turn pro in the summer of 1974. My first play-for-pay experience happened to be a grass court tournament at Newport, Rhode Island, site of the International Tennis Hall of Fame. I surprised everybody, including myself, by advancing all the way to the finals before losing 6-4, 6-4 to — you guessed it — Chris Evert. (Chris had just returned from London, where she had captured her first Wimbledon crown.) After Newport, I thought I could be a *contendah*, as Marlon Brando said in the movie "On the Waterfront."

I contended, but I never pocketed that one Big Win during a pro career that lasted twenty-two years. Still, there were some great moments that I can look back on with pride. I won thirty-five singles and doubles titles in far-flung places like London, Paris, Melbourne, Tokyo, and Hamburg. I made a nice living depositing prize money checks. I played for a Grand Slam championship — the 1978 Australian Open — but lost the finals in two close sets.

I did capture two Grand Slam doubles

titles in Australia and played on Wimbledon's Centre Court for the Ladies' Doubles Championship in 1986, which was a losing effort. I was a Top Ten doubles player in the world rankings and was ranked as high as No. 17 in the world in singles. I scored lifetime wins over Martina Navratilova, Pam Shriver, Arantxa Sanchez-Vicario, and even Chris Evert. My last match was at the 1996 Wimbledon, where I played doubles with my close friend, Monica Seles — a great way to wind up a career.

I was thirty-nine years old when I partnered with Monica, which means that I was positively ancient to our teenage opponents. Little did they know that I was ready for a new "season" — that of motherhood. For several years, I had been thinking about starting a family with my husband, Mark, but I was so clueless that I didn't know my biological clock was ticking like Westminster Abbey's Big Ben — *gong, gong, gong.*

After experiencing years of irregular cycles due to my strenuous athletic activity, I certainly wasn't very calculating regarding the best time to try to *create* a baby. Dr. Lisa Erickson, a friend and an in-vitro specialist, shook me out of my doldrums.

"You have to take a Lear jet, not a Volkswagen, if you're wanting to get pregnant," she said. "I think you have to go for in-vitro now."

I knew she was right. Mark and I had three times tried artificial insemination and failed. A friend from my Bible study group, Betti Gorenflo, had just delivered a beautiful boy, Riley, through in-vitro, so I consulted with Dr. Frank Rigelin Orlando. I became pregnant on my first try in the spring of 1997! The pregnancy proceeded with no complications, and Maggie arrived in this world on December 13, 1997, when I was forty-one years old.

Maggie's birth meant much more to me than holding any trophy aloft on Centre Court. If I had known how enriching parenthood would be, I would have never let my biological clock tick as long as it did. I love motherhood!

I also know this: my memories of professional tennis are fading quickly and losing value with each passing day. It's not that I have any regrets; on the contrary, I now feel the bond between Maggie and me is more important than anything I could have accomplished on the tennis court. I know what is truly important now.

I run into Chris Evert several times a year these days. Those head-to-head scrapes we had on the tennis court have long been forgotten between us. We rarely talk tennis. Instead, we talk about our families. I can tell that her three sons — Alex, Nicky, and Colton — mean more to her than all eighteen Grand Slam singles titles.

I think Chris would agree with me that this great quote from Dr. James Dobson says it all. I hope Dr. Dobson, a former collegiate tennis player, doesn't mind that I've added a few words.

> *"I have concluded that the accumulation of wealth [and tennis titles], even if I could achieve it, is an insufficient reason for living. When I reach the end of my days, a moment or two from now, I must look backward on something more meaningful than the pursuit of houses and land and machines*

and stocks and bonds [and Grand Slam championships]. Nor is fame of any lasting benefit. I will consider my earthly existence to have been wasted unless I can recall a loving family, a consistent investment in the lives of people, and an earnest attempt to serve the God who made me. Nothing else makes much sense."

I strive daily to serve God, my husband, and my daughter.

Tennis is a great game and always will be. But in the end, it's just a game.

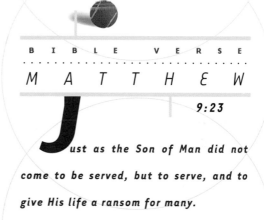

BIBLE VERSE

MATTHEW
9:23

Just as the Son of Man did not come to be served, but to serve, and to give His life a ransom for many.

"GAME, SET, AND MATCH..."

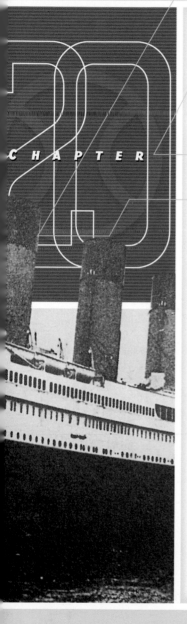

CHAPTER 20

As we have looked at some of the highlights of tennis history, the players that made it great, and the lessons learned along the way, there is one final story I'd like to share.

In 1912, Richard Norris Williams was a young American living in Geneva, Switzerland, when he was accepted to Harvard University. Richard was an accomplished tennis player and looked forward to playing intercollegiate tennis for Harvard.

Traveling from Geneva to the United States in 1912 meant taking a train across France to the port of Cherbourg, where Richard and his father, Charles, boarded a ship bound for America. His father had purchased first-class tickets for a stateroom on the *R.M.S. Titanic*, which was embarking on its maiden voyage to New York.

Four days into her journey across the Atlantic, the *Titanic* struck an iceberg. You know what happened next: there weren't enough lifeboats for the 2,200 passengers, so Captain Edward Smith ordered, "Women and children first," into the lifeboats. Richard and his father were out of luck.

They wandered about the decks as the mighty *Titanic* began listing. They could see the lights of the lifeboats in the distance, and I'm sure they knew what fate awaited them. Feeling the intense cold on the decks, Richard and his dad sought warmth in the ship's gymnasium, where other men without hope were congregating.

The moment of truth came when the *Titanic* foundered and began to sink to its watery grave. By this time, the father and son were back out on the decks. As the *Titanic* rose into the air, its forward funnel collapsed, crushing Charles Williams and many others. Richard dove for the icy water at the last possible instant, and in the resulting chaos, he hung onto a half-submerged collapsible lifeboat. He managed to stay alive until he was plucked out of the freezing water by those in Lifeboat 14.

Richard was suffering terribly from the cold. His legs felt as though they were frozen stiff, but at least he was still breathing. He managed to survive six more hours until another ship, the *Carpathia*, rescued them.

The *Carpathia's* doctor recommended that Richard's legs be amputated, but Richard refused — probably because he was twenty-one years old and feared never walking again, let alone playing tennis. He doggedly exercised his ailing legs, and he miraculously recovered full use of them. He began playing tennis, and just four months later, he reached the quarterfinals of the U.S. Championships (the U.S. Open today) before losing the tournament.

Richard Williams eventually won two U.S. titles — a Wimbledon doubles crown and the gold medal in mixed doubles at the 1924 Olympic Games in Paris. He was elected to the International Tennis Hall of Fame in 1957.

I love this story about Richard Norris Williams and the *Titanic*, because it represents an incredible study of how humans react when faced with certain demise. Imagine what it must have been like to stand on the listing upper deck of the *Titanic* after the last lifeboat had been lowered to the water. Soon, very soon, you would die a horrible death in icy cold water. Knowing that you were standing on the precipice of eternity, would you have fallen to your knees and worshipped the Lord of the universe, or would you have looked to the heavens and cursed God out of anger and bitterness?

John Harper, another *Titanic* passenger who was traveling to Chicago to become the pastor of Moody Memorial Church, stayed with the ship until the very end. When she raised up and slid into the deep, icy waters, Harper jumped free — just like Richard Williams. While thrashing about in the frigid water, Harper won his last convert just before he drowned. The new believer was a young Scotsman who — like Richard Williams — was also one of the few to survive the *Titanic* tragedy.

The Scotsman said Harper clung to a floating spar and called out, "Are ye saved, mon?" and quoted Acts 16:31 ("Believe in the Lord Jesus, and you will be saved") before the frozen seas claimed him.

In the days following the sinking outside the White Star Line office in Liverpool, a great crowd of the passengers' relatives gathered. Two large boards were placed on each side of the entrance. Above each was printed in large letters: KNOWN TO BE SAVED and KNOWN TO BE LOST.

A newspaper account from those days described it like this: "Every now and then, a man would appear from the office bearing a large piece of cardboard on which was written the name of one of the passengers. As he held up the name, a deathly stillness swept over the crowd; it watched to see to which of the boards he would pin the name."

Was the *Titanic* passenger saved or lost? From a spiritual perspective, had that person accepted the free gift of salvation through believing in Jesus Christ? Where was he or she spending eternity? In scripture, the "Romans Road" teaches us everyone has sinned (Rom. 3:23), that the penalty for our sin is death (Rom. 6:23), that Jesus Christ died for our sins (Rom. 5:8), and that to be forgiven for our sins, we must believe and confess that Jesus is Lord because salvation comes only through Jesus Christ (Rom. 10:8–10). Do you know where you will spend eternity? I hope you do. Will you win the game of life, only to lose the overall match? If you are not sure, I invite you to ask Jesus Christ into your life and know that you will spend eternity with Him. Jeremiah 33:3 says, "Call to me and I will answer you," which means we have a direct line to God. If you, at this moment in time, seek to spend eternity with Jesus Christ, I plead with you to please pray this simple prayer right now:

> *Dear Lord Jesus:*
> *I come to You right now . . . and admit that I am a sinner.*
> *I repent of my sins against You. I believe that You died on the*
> *cross for my sins . . . and that You rose again three days later.*
> *I ask that you forgive me . . . and that You come into my life. Amen.*

Did you pray that prayer? If so, great! One day, you'll shake hands with Jesus and hear Him say the best words you'll ever hear: "Well done, my good and faithful servant."

JOHN

3:16

For God so loved the world that He gave His only begotten Son, that whoever believes in Him should not perish but have everlasting life.